特長と使い方

～本書を活用した大学入試対策～

☐ **志望校を決める(調べる・考える)**
　入試日程，受験科目，出題範囲，レベルなどが決まるので，やるべきことが見えやすくなります。

☐ **「合格」までのスケジュールを決める**

　基礎固め・苦手克服期 …受験勉強スタート～入試の 6 か月前頃

　・教科書レベルの問題を解けるようにします。

　・苦手分野をなくしましょう。

　⤷ 教科書レベルの英文法がほぼ理解できている人は，
　　『大学入試 ステップアップ 英文法【標準】』に取り組みましょう。

　応用力養成期 …入試の 6 か月前～ 3 か月前頃

　・身につけた基礎を土台にして，入試レベルの問題に対応できる応用力を養成します。

　・志望校の過去問を確認して，出題傾向，解答の形式などを把握しておきましょう。

　・模試を積極的に活用しましょう。模試で課題などが見つかったら，『大学入試 ステップアップ 英文法【標準】』で復習して，確実に解けるようにしておきましょう。

　実戦力養成期 …入試の 3 か月前頃～入試直前

　・時間配分や解答の形式を踏まえ，できるだけ本番に近い状態で過去問に取り組みましょう。

志望校合格！！

📖 英語の学習法

◎ **同じ問題を何度も繰り返し解く**
　多くの教材に取り組むよりも，1 つの教材を何度も繰り返し解く方が力がつきます。
　⤷『大学入試 ステップアップ 英文法【標準】』の活用例を，次のページで紹介しています。

◎ **解けない問題こそ実力アップのチャンス**
　間違えた問題の解説を読んでも理解できないときは，解説を 1 行ずつ丁寧に理解しながら読むまたは書き写して，自分のつまずき箇所を明確にしましょう。教科書レベルの内容がよく理解できないときは，さらに前に戻って復習することも大切です。

◎ **基本問題は確実に解けるようにする**
　応用問題も基本問題の組み合わせです。まずは基本問題が確実に解けるようにしましょう。解ける基本問題が増えていくことで，応用力も必ず身についてきます。

◎ **ケアレスミス対策**
　日頃から，問題をよく読んで答える習慣を身につけ，実際の試験でも解いた後に再度確認し，ケアレスミスを 1 つでもなくせるように注意しましょう。

～本書のしくみ～

本冊

基本的には，見開き2ページで1単元完結し，必要に応じて見開き4ページ構成で，簡潔かつ明快な英文で構成。

🖐 要点整理
重要事項をまとめています。ひとつひとつ確実に理解し，覚えましょう。

☆ 重要な問題
ぜひ取り組んでおきたい問題です。状況に応じて効率よく学習を進めるときの目安にもなります。

advice
つまずきそうな問題には，適宜ヒントを掲載しています。

解答・解説

解答部分を赤く示し，解説との見分けをつきやすく工夫したので，答え合わせがしやすくなっています。

「解答→解説」の順に配列しているので，大問単位でしっかり理解を深められます。

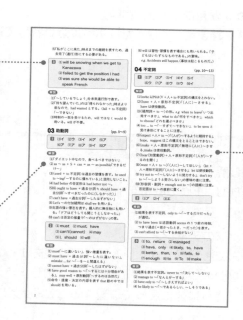

詳しい解説つきです。正誤確認だけでなく，解答するときのポイントになる文法解説も注目しましょう。

📖 本書の活用例

◎ 何度も繰り返し取り組むとき，1巡目は全問→2巡目は1巡目に間違った問題→3巡目は2巡目に間違った問題…のように進めて，全問解けるようになるまで繰り返します。

◎ ざっと全体を復習したいときは，各単元の要点整理だけ取り組むと効率的です。

目　次

Date

01 文と文型 …………………… 4 [　/　] [　/　] [　/　]

02 時　制 …………………… 6 [　/　] [　/　] [　/　]

03 助動詞 …………………… 8 [　/　] [　/　] [　/　]

04 不定詞 …………………… 10 [　/　] [　/　] [　/　]

05 動名詞 …………………… 14 [　/　] [　/　] [　/　]

06 分　詞 …………………… 18 [　/　] [　/　] [　/　]

07 受け身 …………………… 22 [　/　] [　/　] [　/　]

08 比　較 …………………… 24 [　/　] [　/　] [　/　]

09 関係詞 …………………… 26 [　/　] [　/　] [　/　]

10 仮定法 …………………… 30 [　/　] [　/　] [　/　]

11 話法・時制の一致 …………… 32 [　/　] [　/　] [　/　]

12 否　定 …………………… 34 [　/　] [　/　] [　/　]

13 無生物主語・名詞構文 ……… 36 [　/　] [　/　] [　/　]

14 呼応・倒置・強調・省略 …… 38 [　/　] [　/　] [　/　]

15 接続詞 …………………… 40 [　/　] [　/　] [　/　]

16 名詞・冠詞 ……………… 42 [　/　] [　/　] [　/　]

17 代名詞 …………………… 44 [　/　] [　/　] [　/　]

18 形容詞・副詞 …………… 46 [　/　] [　/　] [　/　]

19 句動詞 …………………… 48 [　/　] [　/　] [　/　]

20 前置詞 …………………… 52 [　/　] [　/　] [　/　]

01 | 文と文型

要点整理

❶ 特定の目的語を必要とする動詞

> Would you **mind explaining** that again ? 〔動名詞〕
> My mother **promised to buy** me a new bike. 〔to 不定詞〕
> The doctor **advised him to give** up smoking. 〔V ＋人＋ to 不定詞〕

❷ 特定の前置詞と結びつく動詞

> This picture **reminds** me **of** my high school days.
> The heavy rain **kept** us **from** playing tennis.

❸ It の用法

> **It** was foolish of you to trust him. 〔形式主語〕
> I found **it** impossible to swim across the river. 〔形式目的語〕

❹ 自動詞と他動詞の判別

他動詞の場合はすぐ後に目的語がくるが，自動詞の場合は目的語の前に前置詞が必要。

> We **reached** the hotel at midnight. 〔他動詞〕
> We **arrived** at the hotel at midnight. 〔自動詞〕

❺ いろいろな文型に用いられる動詞

I'm **leaving** for London tomorrow. 〔第１文型〕
My father often **leaves** his *umbrella* on a train. 〔第３文型〕
He **left** his *son* a large *fortune*. 〔第４文型〕
Don't **leave** the *engine running*. 〔第５文型〕

❻ 不定詞の意味上の主語を文の主語にできない形容詞 … necessary / difficult / important

> （正）It　is　difficult **for you** to do it.
> （誤）You are difficult　　　　to do it.

---

1 次の各文の＿＿＿に適当な前置詞を入れよ。何も入らなければ×を書け。

(1) They kept their children ＿＿＿＿＿＿ touching the heater.

(2) It was midnight when we reached ＿＿＿＿＿＿ our destination.

(3) This cottage reminds me ＿＿＿＿＿＿ the one I was born in.

(4) It is kind ＿＿＿＿＿＿ you to show me the way to the station.

(5) My father and my uncle resemble ＿＿＿＿＿＿ each other.

(6) Let's discuss ＿＿＿＿＿＿ the question tomorrow.

(7) You must apologize ＿＿＿＿＿＿ Mr. Smith for being late.

☆ **2** 次のア〜カのうち，文法的に誤りのあるものを２つ選び，記号で答えよ。

ア Shall I get you the magazine on the table?

イ We found it difficult to answer the question.

ウ I said my husband to turn on the light of the dining room.

エ David finally persuaded his sister to go to see a doctor.

オ This jacket will become you very well.

カ Would you mind to bring me my suitcase?　　　　　　　　（　　）（　　）

3 次の各文の下線部の誤りを正せ。

(1) You are necessary to read this book.　　　　　　　　　　　　　　［西南学院大］

_____

(2) This is the castle at which I visited three years ago.

_____

(3) Such a book is no use reading.　　　　　　　　　　　　　　　　　［立教大］

_____

(4) I will explain you the meaning.　　　　　　　　　　　　　　　　［國學院大］

_____

(5) When are you convenient to come over here?　　　　　　　　　　［関西学院大］

_____

4 次の各文の（　）内に，語法的に適当なものをすべて選び，記号で答えよ。

(1) The dish you are cooking smells (　　　　). 　　　　　　　　　　［名城大-改］

　　ア delicious　　　イ deliciously　　　ウ like delicious　　　エ なし

(2) I promised (　　　) for him.

　　ア to vote　　　イ voting　　　ウ that I would vote　　　エ なし

(3) I enjoy (　　　) on such a sunny day.

　　ア to ski　　　イ skiing　　　ウ that I ski　　　エ なし

(4) English grammar (　　　) me a lot.　　　　　　　　　　　　　　［杏林大-改］

　　ア interests　　　イ interesting　　　ウ interested in　　　エ なし

(5) She introduced (　　　).

　　ア George for me　　イ George to me　　ウ me George　　エ なし

(6) She tried (　　　) more careful.

　　ア to be　　　イ being　　　ウ that she was　　　エ なし

(7) The teacher ordered Taro (　　　) his homework.　　　　　　　［日本大-改］

　　ア to submit　　　イ submits　　　ウ submitted　　　エ なし

advice
2 カ mind「気にする，いやだと思う」
3 (1) necessary は to 不定詞の意味上の主語を，文の主語にとれない。

5

02 | 時　制

🖰 要点整理

❶ 現在時制の注意すべき表現

時・条件を表す副詞節では**未来形を用いずに現在形を用いる**。

> *If* it **rains** tomorrow, we won't go on a picnic.

真理・現在の習慣は時制の一致を受けない。

> Our teacher *told* us that the earth **goes** round the sun.

❷ 過去時制に関する注意すべき表現

現在完了と同じく，**ever，never** を伴って**経験**を表す。

> **Did** you *ever* **hear** of such a strange custom ?

過去完了の代用　前後関係が明らかな場合，過去完了を用いる必要がない。

> *After* we **finished** dinner, we *went* on talking.

❸ 未来時制に関する注意すべき表現

will には，未来を表す用法以外に，**習慣，習性**を表す用法もある。

> Children **will** be noisy.（子どもはうるさいものだ。）

その他の未来の表現　**be going to ～，be about to ～**

❹ 現在完了に関する注意すべき表現

過去の１点を明確に表す語句(yesterday，two weeks ago など)とは一緒に用いられない。

> When *have* you *bought* (→ did you buy) the dictionary ?

時・条件を表す**副詞節**では，**未来完了を用いずに現在完了を用いる**。

> I'll go home *when* I **have finished** this task.

❺ 過去完了に関する注意すべき表現

過去の一定時までの**経験，状態の継続，動作・状態の完了・結果**を表す。

> He **had been** ill for a week *when* the doctor was sent for.

❻ 未来完了に関する注意すべき表現

未来の一定時(まで)における**完了・結果・経験・継続**を表す。

> We **will have lived** here for three years *by* next March.

❼ 進行形に関する注意すべき表現

一般的に**進行形をとらない動詞**　belong，consist，resemble，want など。

1 次の各文の(　)内に下から適当なものを選び，記号で答えよ。

⑴ "John smokes too much." "Well, he used to smoke more than he (　　　) now."

　ア does　　　　**イ** did　　　　**ウ** could　　　　**エ** has

☆ (2) The picture on the wall is shiny. It must (　　　　) quite recently.　　　[共立女子大]

　　　ア be painted　　　イ have been painted　　　ウ have painted　　　エ paint

(3) Last week there (　　　　) a big festival in our town.　　　[(3)・(4)名古屋商大]

　　　ア is　　　　　　イ had　　　　　　ウ has　　　　　　エ was

(4) He (　　　　) when the telephone rang.

　　　ア is sleeping　　　イ sleeps　　　ウ will sleep　　　エ was sleeping

☆ (5) Will you please lend me the book when you (　　　　) it ?　　　[別府大]

　　　ア finished　　　イ have finished　　　ウ will finish

☆ (6) I (　　　　) waited long before she turned up.　　　[駒澤大]

　　　ア had not　　　イ have not　　　ウ should not be　　　エ having not

☆ (7) Let's go home before it (　　　　).　　　[玉川大]

　　　ア will rain　　　イ won't rain　　　ウ rains　　　エ doesn't rain

☆ (8) My mother (　　　　) well by the time spring comes round.

　　　ア got　　　イ has got　　　ウ had got　　　エ will have got

2 次の各文の下線部のうち，文法的に誤りのあるものを１つ選び，記号で答えよ。

(1) If she ア<u>will come</u> in my イ<u>absence</u>, please tell ウ<u>her to</u> エ<u>come back</u> this evening.

　　　　　　　　　　　　　　　　　　　　　　　　　　　　　　[桜美林大-改]

　　　　　　　　　　　　　　　　　　　　　　　　　　　　（　　　　）

(2) We ア<u>know</u> each イ<u>other</u> ウ<u>since</u> we were six エ<u>years</u> old.　　　[中京大]

　　　　　　　　　　　　　　　　　　　　　　　　　　　　（　　　　）

(3) ア<u>Your way</u> イ<u>of telling</u> stories ウ<u>is resembling</u> エ<u>your teacher's</u> very much.　　　[近畿大-改]

　　　　　　　　　　　　　　　　　　　　　　　　　　　　（　　　　）

(4) ア<u>When</u> イ<u>has</u> the express train ウ<u>for</u> Osaka come エ<u>to</u> the platform ?　　　（　　　　）

(5) ア<u>I have been studying</u> English in Japan イ<u>for</u> ウ<u>nearly</u> ten years before I エ<u>came</u> here.

　　　　　　　　　　　　　　　　　　　　　　　　　　　　[明治学院大]

　　　　　　　　　　　　　　　　　　　　　　　　　　　　（　　　　）

3 日本語を参考に，（　）内の語句を並べかえよ。

(1) 金沢に着くころには，雪が降っているでしょう。　　　[金沢工業大]

　　It (be / get / Kanazawa / snowing / to / we / when / will).

　　It ＿＿＿＿＿＿＿＿＿＿＿＿＿＿＿＿＿＿＿＿＿＿＿＿＿＿＿＿＿＿.

(2) 私は待ち望んでいた地位を得られなかった。　　　[京都女子大]

　　I (to / had / get / position / failed / the / I) wanted.

　　I ＿＿＿＿＿＿＿＿＿＿＿＿＿＿＿＿＿＿＿＿＿＿＿＿ wanted.

(3) レベッカは自分がフランス語を話せるようになるという確信があった。

　　Rebecca (will / sure / French / able / to / she / be / was / speak / would). 〔１語不要〕

　　Rebecca ＿＿＿＿＿＿＿＿＿＿＿＿＿＿＿＿＿＿＿＿＿＿＿＿＿＿.

03 | 助動詞

月　　日

解答 ▶ 別冊p.2

🖑 要点整理

❶ 主語の意志・拒絶を表す … will（現在），would（過去）

> She **would not** listen to my advice.

❷ 現在・過去の習慣を表す … will，would

> He **would** often spend the whole weekend listening to records.

❸ can

疑問文では**強い疑い**を，否定文では**強い否定的推量**を表すことがある。

> That **can't** be Bob — he's in New York.（あれはボブのはずがない）

❹ that 節で使われる should

ⓐ It is *strange* that you **should** trust such a dishonest man.〔感情の原因〕

ⓑ It is *necessary* that you **should** see a doctor at once.〔当然・必要の表現〕

ⓒ He *suggested* that the meeting **should** be put off.〔命令・提案・決定の表現〕

❺ 強い推量を表す must

〔反対の意味は ❸ の **can't** で表す。〕

> Jane **must** be in her twenties.（ジェーンは 20 代に違いない。）

❻ must の否定形 … don't have to，don't need to，need not

> **Must** we wait till you come back ?

　— **Yes**, you **must**. / — **No**, you **don't have to**〔**don't need to**，**need not**〕.

❼ 義務・当然を表す … ought to（≒ should）

> **Ought** I **to** go to a dentist ? — Yes, you **ought to**.

❽ 過去の規則的習慣，状態を表す …〈used ＋ to 不定詞〉

> There **used to** be a bookshop around here.

❾ 慣用表現

may as well「〜してもよいだろう」，**would rather 〜 than ...**「…よりむしろ〜したい」，**may well**「〜するのは当然だ」，**had better**「〜したほうがよい」**否定語は原形動詞の直前につける。** *e.g.* had better **not** 〜

❿ 助動詞＋ have ＋過去分詞

must have ＋過去分詞「〜したに違いない」，may have ＋過去分詞「〜したかもしれない」，cannot have ＋過去分詞「〜したはずがない」，should〔ought to〕have ＋過去分詞「当然〜したはずだ」または「〜すべきであったのに」，need not have ＋過去分詞「〜する必要はなかったのに」

☆ **1** 次の各文の（　）内に下から適当なものを選び，記号で答えよ。

(1) "Would you like some cake ?" "Yes, please, though I (　　　) not eat it really as I'm on a diet."

　　ア would　　　　イ should　　　　ウ could　　　　エ do

(2) He said to me, "Please be as quiet as you (　　　)."

　　ア should　　　　イ could　　　　ウ can　　　　エ have

(3) I (　　　) to bed after midnight because my favorite program started at 11:00.　［京都産業大］

　　ア am used to go　　イ used to go　　ウ used to going　　エ use to go

(4) You had (　　　) keep company with him.　　　　　　　　　　　　　　　　［立命館大］

　　ア better not　　　イ better not to　　　ウ not better　　　エ not better to

(5) The picture was wonderful. You (　　　) to have seen it.

　　ア ought　　　　イ should　　　　ウ have　　　　エ had

(6) I (　　　) Mr. Patterson this afternoon, but I forgot.　　　　　　　　　　［日本大］

　　ア should have phoned　　　イ should phone

　　ウ will have phoned　　　　エ will phone

(7) Since everybody believes he is as good as his word, he (　　　) have broken any promise.　　　　　　　　　　　　　　　　　　　　　　　　　　　　　　　　　　［昭和女子大］

　　ア can't　　　　イ might　　　　ウ mustn't　　　　エ should

(8) Let's start early in the morning, (　　　)?　　　　　　　　　　　　　　　［同志社大］

　　ア shall we　　　イ do we　　　ウ don't you　　　エ don't we

(9) Something was wrong with the door; it (　　　) not open.　　　　　　　　　［福岡大］

　　ア will　　　　イ would　　　　ウ shall　　　　エ should

(10) She (　　　) be over thirty; she must still be in her twenties.

　　ア can't　　　　イ may　　　　ウ must　　　　エ oughtn't

☆ **2** 次の各組の英文がほぼ同じ内容になるように，＿＿＿に適当な語を入れよ。

(1) ⎰ It is certain that Steve is interested in the fact.　　　　　　　　　　　　［立正大］
　　 ⎱ Steve ＿＿＿＿＿＿ be interested in the fact.

(2) ⎰ I am sure he mistook me for my sister.　　　　　　　　　　［神戸松蔭女子学院大］
　　 ⎱ He ＿＿＿＿＿＿ ＿＿＿＿＿＿ mistaken me for my sister.

(3) ⎰ It is impossible that she should have done such a thing.　　　　　　　　［九州女子大］
　　 ⎱ She ＿＿＿＿＿＿ have done such a thing.

(4) ⎰ She has good reason to get angry.　　　　　　　　　　　　　　　　　　［亜細亜大］
　　 ⎱ She ＿＿＿＿＿＿ well get angry.

(5) ⎰ Josh said to me, "Please send me a Christmas card."
　　 ⎱ Josh requested that ＿＿＿＿＿＿ ＿＿＿＿＿＿ send him a Christmas card.

(6) ⎰ It is natural for children to be naughty.
　　 ⎱ Children ＿＿＿＿＿＿ be naughty.

04 | 不定詞

👆 要点整理

❶ to 不定詞の基本的用法

ⓐ 名詞用法，ⓑ 形容詞用法，ⓒ 副詞用法

ⓐ **To learn** a new language is difficult.

ⓑ I have nothing particular **to do** today.

ⓒ I've come here **to have** a talk with you.〔目的〕

　 The boy grew up **to be** a great statesman.〔結果〕

　 I'm very happy **to see** you.〔感情の原因・理由〕

❷ 完了不定詞

〈**to have ＋過去分詞**〉で，述語動詞よりも前の「時」を表す。

> He *is* said **to have been** seriously ill.

　 ＝ It *is* said that he **was** seriously ill.

> He *was* said **to have been** seriously ill.

　 ＝ It *was* said that he **had been** seriously ill.

❸ 原形不定詞

ⓐ 知覚動詞と共に用いる。ⓑ 使役動詞と共に用いる。

ⓐ We never *heard* him **speak** so rudely.

　 ＝ He *was* never *heard* **to speak** so rudely.〔受動態〕

ⓑ The teacher *made* him **stay** in after school.

　 ＝ He *was made* **to stay** in after school by the teacher.〔受動態〕

❹ 慣用的独立不定詞

strange to say「妙な話だが」，to make matters worse「さらに悪いことに」，to say nothing of ～「～は言うまでもなく」，to begin with「まず第一に」，needless to say「言うまでもなく」，to tell the truth「実を言うと」

❺ 慣用表現

> I hurried to the station **in order〔so as〕to catch** the express.（～するために）

　 ＝ I hurried to the station *in order〔so〕that* I *could* catch the express.

> This parcel is **too** heavy *for* me **to carry**.（～すぎて…できない）

　 ＝ This parcel is so heavy *that I cannot carry* it.

> He was **so kind as to lend** me some money.（とても～なので…）

　 ＝ He was kind **enough to lend** me some money.

> **All** you **have to do is (to) work** hard.（～しさえすればよい）

　 ＝ You **have only to work** hard.

1 次の各文の（　）内に下から適当なものを選び，記号で答えよ。

(1) They (　　　) me to play cards. ［京都産業大］

  ア invited イ offered ウ showed エ suggested

☆ (2) Please have the porter (　　　) these suitcases to my room.

  ア take イ to take ウ taking エ taken

(3) The question is which (　　　). ［南山大］

  ア choose イ to choose ウ choosing エ chosen

☆ (4) He is too proud (　　　) in public with his poorly dressed father.

  ア to see イ to be seen ウ of being seen

  エ of seeing オ having been seen

(5) She is very intelligent. I (　　　) her to pass the examination easily. ［神戸女学院大］

  ア hope イ expect ウ suggest エ desire

☆ (6) Tom suggested that I make (　　　) my grade since I was sick the day of the examination.

  ア the teacher to change イ the teacher changing

  ウ the teacher change エ the teacher to be changing

(7) I heard her (　　　) English fluently. ［千葉商科大］

  ア speak イ speaks ウ spoke エ to speak

(8) I want you (　　　) what time will be convenient for you.

  ア let me know   イ let me to know

  ウ to let me know   エ to let me to know

(9) "Would you like another cup of tea?" ［京都女子大］

  "No, thanks. I (　　　) more than one cup a day."

  ア try to have   イ try to have any

  ウ try not to have   エ don't try to have

☆ (10) He was wise (　　　) drive when he was feeling ill.

  ア not enough to   イ enough not to

  ウ to not enough   エ enough to not

2 次の各組の英文がほぼ同じ内容になるように，（　）内に下から適当なものを選び，記号で答えよ。

［桜美林大-改］

(1) ⎰ My mother went to see the doctor, but she found him absent.

  ⎱ My mother went to see the doctor, (　　　) find him absent.

  ア only to   イ about to

  ウ in order to   エ enough to

(2) $\begin{cases} \text{Yuri seems to have been very smart when she was young.} \\ \text{It seems that Yuri (\quad) very smart when she was young.} \end{cases}$ [桜美林大]

　　ア has been　　　　　　イ was
　　ウ had been　　　　　　エ is

(3) $\begin{cases} \text{We don't have enough money to support you all the way through college.} \\ \text{We (\quad) to support you all the way through college.} \end{cases}$ [亜細亜大-改]

　　ア are not willing　　　　　イ should not have the power
　　ウ are not rich so as　　　　エ cannot afford

3 次の各組の英文がほぼ同じ内容になるように，＿＿＿に適当な語を入れよ。

(1) $\begin{cases} \text{The good old days are gone and will never return.} \\ \text{The good old days are gone, never _____ _____.} \end{cases}$ [中央大]

(2) $\begin{cases} \text{I somehow finished the book.} \\ \text{I _____ to finish the book.} \end{cases}$

☆(3) $\begin{cases} \text{All you have to do is to study hard.} \\ \text{You _____ _____ to study hard.} \end{cases}$ [日本文化大]

(4) $\begin{cases} \text{It is likely that he has already gone.} \\ \text{He is _____ _____ _____ already gone.} \end{cases}$

☆(5) $\begin{cases} \text{She is not so foolish as to make such a mistake.} \\ \text{She knows _____ _____ _____ make such a mistake.} \end{cases}$

(6) $\begin{cases} \text{She comes to see me every Sunday.} \\ \text{She never _____ _____ come to see me on Sunday.} \end{cases}$ [獨協大]

☆(7) $\begin{cases} \text{Would you be so kind as to lend me your book ?} \\ \text{Would you be kind _____ to lend me your book ?} \end{cases}$ [明治大]

(8) $\begin{cases} \text{We could not see anyone in the street.} \\ \text{No one was _____ be seen in the street.} \end{cases}$ [亜細亜大]

☆(9) $\begin{cases} \text{If you heard him talk, you would take him for an American.} \\ \text{_____ hear him talk, you would take him for an American.} \end{cases}$

(10) $\begin{cases} \text{What is worse, he has been ill in bed.} \\ \text{To _____ matters worse, he has been ill in bed.} \end{cases}$

advice
3 (4) likely 「〜しそうである，たぶん〜するだろう」

4 次の各文の下線部のうち，文法的に誤りのあるものを 1 つ選び，記号で答えよ。

(1) ァYou are not ィallowed ゥsmoking in any ェplace in this building. [桜美林大]

（　　）

(2) We must adjust our ァway of life to ィeffective reduce global warming ゥby limiting greenhouse gas emissions ェinto the atmosphere. [立命館大]

（　　）

(3) The book about ァChinese history ィis said ゥto be published ェin the18th century. [近畿大-改]

（　　）

(4) When Mary was seen ァdance ィexcitedly on the stage, everyone ゥthought that she looked ェlike a professional dancer. [福島大-改]

（　　）

(5) ァFor more than a year, Prof. White has been trying to ィmake her shy students to ゥvoice their opinions ェin class. [松山大]

（　　）

(6) When George was young, he ァwould say that he wanted to be a film actor. After ィgraduating from high school, he ゥmade great efforts, and finally he got ェa chance to acting in a movie. [愛知学院大]

（　　）

☆ **5** 日本語を参考に，（　）内の語句を並べかえよ。

(1) 彼女は休暇のためのお金を十分貯めるために懸命に働いた。 [明海大-改]

She worked very hard (enough / to / in / order / save / money / for) a holiday.

She worked very hard ＿＿＿＿＿＿＿＿＿＿＿＿＿＿＿＿＿＿＿＿＿＿＿＿＿ a holiday.

(2) 彼らはその事件とは何の関係もなかったふりをしている。 [日本大-改]

They (do / had / have / pretend / to / with / nothing / to) the affair.

They ＿＿＿＿＿＿＿＿＿＿＿＿＿＿＿＿＿＿＿＿＿＿＿＿＿＿＿＿ the affair.

(3) 私を見送りにわざわざ駅まで来てくれてありがとう。 [日本大-改]

It's (all / of / come / nice / way / you / to / the) to the station to see me off.

It's ＿＿＿＿＿＿＿＿＿＿＿＿＿＿＿＿＿＿＿＿＿＿＿＿＿ to the station to see me off.

05 | 動名詞

☞ 要点整理

❶ 動名詞の基本用法

ⓐ主語，ⓑ動詞の目的語，ⓒ前置詞の目的語，ⓓ補語として用いられる。

ⓐ **Being** honest all the time is not always easy.

ⓑ Did you *finish* **painting** your house?

ⓒ *In spite of* **traveling** alone, she enjoyed her vacation.

ⓓ One of my bad habits *is* **biting** my nails.

❷ 完了動名詞

〈having ＋過去分詞〉の形で，述語動詞より「前」の時を表す。

> I *regret* **not having seen** the show.

　= I *regret* that I *did not see* the show.

❸ 動名詞の意味上の主語

動名詞の直前に，所有格または目的格を置いて表す。

> Would you mind **my〔me〕opening** the window?

　= Would you mind if *I open* the window?

❹ 慣用表現

> **On entering** the house, he took off his hat.

　= *As soon as* he *entered* the house, he took off his hat.

> **There is no telling** what may happen next.

　= *It is impossible to tell* what may happen next.

> I **cannot help laughing** at the sight.

　= I *cannot but laugh* at the sight.

> I don't **feel like eating** a big meal now. （～したい気がする）

> This book is **worth reading**. （～する価値がある）

> We **had** a lot of **difficulty (in) finding** a parking place. （～するのに苦労する）

❺ 動名詞のみを目的語にとる動詞

avoid「避ける」, consider「熟考する」, deny「否定する」, enjoy「楽しむ」, finish「終える」, give up「あきらめる」, mind「気にする」, practice「練習する」など。

★ **1** 次の各文の（　）内に下から適当なものを選び，記号で答えよ。

[(1)～(2)神戸松蔭女子学院大]

(1) There is no (　　　) spoilt children.
　ア satisfied　　　イ satisfy　　　ウ satisfying　　　エ satisfaction

(2) The film is worth (　　　).
　ア to be seen　　　イ seen　　　ウ seeing　　　エ to see

[流通経済大]

(3) She enjoyed (　　　) a walk in the park.
　ア take　　　イ took　　　ウ to take　　　エ taking

[東京電機大]

(4) Mrs. Young wouldn't mind (　　　) in on her unexpectedly.
　ア drop　　　イ me to drop　　　ウ my dropping　　　エ dropping me

[鶴見大]

(5) It's no use (　　　) with him.
　ア arguing　　　イ for argue　　　ウ argue　　　エ argument

[駒澤大]

(6) I am looking forward to (　　　) you next weekend.
　ア be seeing　　　イ having seen　　　ウ see　　　エ seeing

[獨協大]

(7) (　　　) being idle made the teacher angry.
　ア Him　　　イ For him　　　ウ His　　　エ He's

[(8)～(9)上智大]

(8) This car needs (　　　).
　ア to repair　　　イ repairing　　　ウ having repaired

(9) I object (　　　) like that.
　ア to being treated　　　イ to be treated　　　ウ to be treating

[早稲田大]

(10) She has been busy (　　　) for the coming trip to the U.S.
　ア at preparation　　　イ from preparation
　ウ to be prepared　　　エ preparing

2 次の各組の英文がほぼ同じ内容になるように，＿＿に適当な語を入れよ。

[三重中京大]

(1) ⎰ I have no doubt that he will keep his promise.
　 ⎱ I have no doubt of his ＿＿＿＿＿ promise.

[大阪大谷大]

★ (2) ⎰ I have no appetite at all.
　　 ⎱ I don't feel ＿＿＿＿＿ eating at all.

★ (3) ⎰ It was easy for me to find his house.
　　 ⎱ I had ＿＿＿＿＿ difficulty in ＿＿＿＿＿ his house.

(4) ⎰ I'm sure that he will succeed in the entrance exam.
　 ⎱ I'm sure ＿＿＿＿＿ his ＿＿＿＿＿ in the entrance exam.

☆ (5) ⎰ It is needless to say that health is above wealth.   [立命館大]
    ⎱ It goes _____ _____ that health is above wealth.

3 日本語を参考に，（ ）内の語句を並べかえよ。

(1) ビザを取得するのに苦労しましたか。   [駒澤大]

Did you (any / getting / have / difficulty) a visa ?

Did you _____ a visa ?

(2) どちらのチームが勝つのか，予断をゆるさない。   [九州国際大]

There is (team / will / no / win / which / telling) the game.

There is _____ the game.

(3) 日本の子どもたちはお金を稼ぐために雑用をすることに慣れていない。   [愛知工業大-改]

Japanese children (doing / to / are / chores / not / used) to make money.

Japanese children _____ to make money.

4 次の各文の下線部のうち，文法的に誤りのあるものを１つ選び，記号で答えよ。

(1) After ァfailed the examination, George was advised ィthat he ゥcome to school for ェhelp.

    [専修大]

(   )

(2) I ァhad forgotten ィreserving a ticket for the ゥsleeping car, so I had to ェstay at a hotel that night.   (   )

(3) Nancy is proud ァof ィher son ゥto have ェwon the inter-high-school tennis championship last year.   [摂南大-改]

(   )

(4) Susie ァtried ィto eat the cake, but it tasted awful. She ゥregretted ェhaving eaten it.

(   )

(5) The play was so ァboring. I could ィhardly keep myself ゥfor ェfalling asleep.

    [東京理科大-改]

(   )

(6) ァIn addition to ィcause certain types of cancers, ゥsmoking cigarettes is also becoming a very expensive habit ェas well.   [青山学院大]

(   )

advice

4 (6) in addition to ～は「～に加えて」の意味。この to は前置詞。

5 次の各文の下線部の誤りを正せ。

(1) I remember once to learn by heart the names of all the capital cities of the world.

[名城大-改]

_____

★ (2) He can be very rude, but I cannot help to like him.

_____

(3) My computer doesn't work well. It needs to repair.

_____

★ (4) Don't forget mailing the letter on your way to school.

_____

(5) She is busy to cook the dinner.　　　　　　[神戸市外国語大-改]

_____

6 日本語を参考に，（　）内の語句を並べかえよ。

(1) 私はとても遅く帰宅したので，父に叱られた。　　　　　[九州女子大]

Father scolded (for / me / coming / so / home / late).

Father scolded _____.

(2) パスポートを拝見してもかまいませんか。

Would (passport / your / showing / my / you / mind / me)? (1語不要)

Would _____?

(3) 彼女が引っ越すとすぐに彼女の家は売られた。(1語不要)

Her house (sold / soon / was / her / on / moving).

Her house _____.

(4) 日本の列車は安全で時間どおりに運行されることで世界的に有名である。　　　[立命館大]

Japanese trains are (safe / on / being / running / for / world-famous / and) time.

Japanese trains are _____ time.

(5) 彼を気の毒に思わずにいられない。　　　　　[広島経済大]

I (for / cannot / feeling / help / sorry) him.

I _____ him.

06 | 分　詞

✋ 要点整理

❶ 現在分詞と過去分詞

分詞が名詞を修飾するとき，ⓐ単独のときは名詞の前，ⓑ他の語句を伴うときは名詞の後ろに置く。

ⓐ **Barking** *dogs* don't always bite.

　The breeze came through the **broken** *window*.

ⓑ The *girl* **making the most noise** is my sister.

　The *boy* **injured by the bullet** was taken to the hospital.

❷ 補語となる分詞

ⓐ S＋V＋分詞，ⓑ S＋V＋O＋分詞，ⓒ S＋have〔get〕＋O＋過去分詞

ⓐ I *sat* **smoking** and **wondering** what to do.

　My mother *looked* **surprised** at the news.

ⓑ I'm sorry I've *kept* you **waiting**.

　He was able to *make* himself **heard** by shouting.

ⓒ She *had* her new bicycle **stolen**.

　I must *get* my car **repaired**.

❸ 分詞構文の注意すべき用法

(1)　分詞の表す「時」が，文の動詞より前の「時」を表す場合は，〈**having＋過去分詞**〉の形になる。

　　＞ **Having lost** all my money, I *went* home.

　　　＝ *As* I *had lost* all my money, I *went* home.

(2)　**分詞の否定語**はその直前に置く。

　　＞ ***Never*** **having lived** away from home, he will get homesick.

　　　＝ **As** he **has never lived** away from home, he will get homesick.

(3)　分詞の意味上の主語と文の主語が異なる場合は，**分詞の主語は省略できない。**

　　＞ ***It* being** rainy, I could not go hiking.

　　　＝ *As it was* rainy, I could not go hiking.

❹ 慣用的独立分詞構文

＞ **Generally speaking**, the Japanese are a diligent people. （一般的に言って）

＞ **Judging from** the look of the sky, it will rain tomorrow. （～から判断すると）

＞ **Talking of** papers, have you read today's paper？（～と言えば）

1 次の各文の（ ）内に下から適当なものを選び，記号で答えよ。

(1) I haven't (　　　) for a long time. [高知大]

  ア my hair cut   イ had cut my hair

  ウ been cut my hair   エ had my hair cut

(2) She seems (　　　) at the result of the game. [山梨学院大-改]

  ア pleasure   イ pleased   ウ pleasant   エ pleasing

(3) I'm sorry to have kept you (　　　) so long.

  ア wait   イ to wait   ウ waited   エ waiting

(4) Not (　　　) attention, Janet picked up the wrong key. [青山学院大]

  ア to pay   イ pay   ウ paying   エ paid

(5) His friend wants to work for a company (　　　) from Germany. [摂南大]

  ア importing cars   イ it imports cars   ウ imports cars   エ imported cars

(6) Our neighbors had to sweep up the (　　　) leaves from the street in the morning. [佛教大]

  ア fall   イ fallen   ウ falling   エ falls

(7) He could not make himself (　　　) in the noisy hall. [拓殖大]

  ア hear   イ to hear   ウ heard   エ hearing

(8) Weather (　　　), I will go to Mt.Fuji. [杏林大]

  ア good   イ bad   ウ permitting   エ providing

(9) The woman (　　　) in black is a famous actress. [拓殖大]

  ア being dressing   イ dress   ウ dressed   エ dresses

(10) He was sitting on the sofa with his legs (　　　). [摂南大]

  ア crossing   イ to be crossed   ウ crossed   エ having crossed

(11) (　　　) in Guam for a long time, she is used to the tropical climate. [日本大]

  ア Living   イ Lived   ウ Having lived   エ Have lived

2 次の各文の下線部の誤りを正せ。

(1) <u>A drowned man</u> will catch at a straw.

_____

(2) <u>Deeply shocking</u>, I decided never to speak to her again.

_____

(3) <u>Having not read</u> the book, I can't tell whether it's worth reading.

_____

(4) <u>It was Sunday</u>, the library was closed.

_____

(5) We often <u>hear it says</u> that honesty is the best policy.

_____

3 日本語を参考に，____に適当な語を入れよ。

(1) あれこれ考えて，やはり我々はその計画を実行することに決めた。

_____ things _____, we finally decided to carry out the project.

☆ (2) 食べ物と言えば，昼食は何がいいですか。

_____ _____ food, what do you want to have for lunch ?

4 次の各組の英文がほぼ同じ内容になるように，____に適当な語を入れよ。

☆ (1) { As he did not know what to do, he asked me to help.　　　　［大阪大谷大］
    { _____ _____ what to do, he asked me to help.

(2) { To be frank with you, I don't want to join the party.　　　　［福山大］
    { _____ speaking, I don't want to take part _____ the party.

☆ (3) { We found that he was lying on the bed.
    { We found _____ _____ on the bed.

☆ (4) { Even if we admit what you say, we still believe that you are in the wrong.
    { _____ what you say, we still believe that you are in the wrong.

(5) { As there was nothing to do, we went home.
    { _____ _____ _____ to do, we went home.

advice
2 (3)分詞を否定する not は分詞の直前。

5 次の各文の（　）内の動詞を最も適当な形にせよ。

(1) We had Chinese food (deliver) for dinner last night.　　　　　　　　[追手門学院大-改]

_____

☆ (2) The man (injure) in the accident was taken to the hospital.

_____

(3) It was the most (bore) afternoon I could remember.　　　　　　　　[大阪産業大-改]

_____

☆ (4) (Judge) from his expression, he's in a bad mood.

_____

☆ (5) I glanced at the man (seat) next to me.

_____

(6) It (be) cold, you should wear an overcoat.

_____

6 日本語を参考に，（　）内の語句を並べかえよ。

(1) 父は古本をたくさん買ってきた。

My father (of / books / a / bought / used / lot).

My father _____.

(2) ある朝目覚めてみると，ドアが開けっぱなしになっているのがわかった。　　　　　　[近畿大-改]

I awoke one morning (discover / remained / that / the door / to / unclosed).

I awoke one morning _____.

(3) 昨年に比べて，今年は春の訪れが早かった。　　　　　　[専修大]

Spring has come (year / compared / with / than / this / early / ,) last. (1 語不要)

Spring has come _____ last.

(4) 私は英語で何とか理解されるようジェスチャーを交えながら頑張った。　　　　　　[九州産業大]

I tried my best to (myself / in / make / understood / English) using gestures.

I tried my best to _____ using gestures.

(5) 僕は昨日，虫歯を抜いてもらった。

I (a / bad / had / pulled / tooth / out) yesterday.

I _____ yesterday.

advice ....
5 (5) seat oneself = be seated で「腰かける」の意味。

要点整理

❶ S + V + O + O の文の受動態

> My uncle **gave** *me an expensive computer.*
>   → *I* **was given** *an expensive computer* by my uncle.
>   → *An expensive computer* **was given** (to) *me* by my uncle.

❷ 句動詞の受動態

句動詞(laugh at, look up to, take care of など)の受動態は，句動詞を分解できない。

> Everyone *looks up to* the old man.（みんなその老人を尊敬している。）
>   → The old man **is *looked up to*** by everyone.

❸ 注意すべき受動態

> *They*〔*People*〕*say* that she was a beauty in her youth.
>   → **It is said** that she was a beauty in her youth.
>   → She **is said** *to have been* a beauty in her youth.

❹ by 以外の前置詞を用いる受動態（特に感情を表す場合に多く見られる）

> His name **is known *to*** young people.
> We **were caught *in*** a shower on our way home.
> She **was** greatly **disappointed *with*** her son's failure.

☆ **1** 次の各文の（　）内に下から適当なものを選び，記号で答えよ。

(1) The largest cinema （　　　　） in the middle of Eastpark Mall.　　　　[名城大]
　ア locates
　ウ is locating
　イ is located
　エ is being located

(2) The door is （　　　　）.　　　　[愛知工業大]
　ア been painted
　ウ being painted
　イ been painting
　エ being painting

(3) He seldom speaks unless （　　　　）.　　　　[名城大]
　ア he is speaking
　ウ he is spoken to
　イ he is spoken
　エ speaking to

(4) Our professor is known （　　　　） his teaching skills.　　　　[関西学院大-改]
　ア as　　　　**イ** in　　　　**ウ** for　　　　**エ** to

(5) She was (　　　) at the news.

ア shock　　　　　イ shocked　　　　ウ shocking　　　エ to shock

[(5)・(6)日本大]

(6) How many passengers were (　　　) in that train accident?

ア hurtful　　　　イ wounding　　　ウ injured　　　エ damaged

[杏林大]

(7) I cannot believe that many students in my class (　　　) by their first names.

ア prefer being called　　　　　　イ prefer called

ウ rather to be calling　　　　　　エ rather called

[愛知学院大]

(8) When Bob fell down, he was (　　　) all his friends.

ア laughed at　　　イ laughed by　　　ウ laughed　　　エ laughed at by

[創価大]

(9) Cleopatra (　　　) the most beautiful woman in the world.

ア said to be　　　　　　　　　イ said to have been

ウ was said to have been　　　　エ was said to have had been

[法政大]

(10) My car has disappeared. It (　　　).

ア must be stolen　　　　　　　イ must be stealing

ウ must have been stolen　　　エ must have been stealing

2 日本語を参考に，＿＿＿に適当な語を入れよ。

[名古屋女子大]

(1) その会議は1週間おきに開かれる。

The meetings are ＿＿＿＿＿＿ every ＿＿＿＿＿＿ week.

[別府大]

(2) 彼の約束は少しも当てにならない。

His promise cannot be ＿＿＿＿＿＿ on at all.

3 次の各文の下線部のうち，文法的に誤りのあるものを1つ選び，記号で答えよ。

(1) The English literature homework must ア<u>submit</u> to the professor's office イ<u>by the first</u> Monday of ウ<u>each</u> month.

[愛知学院大]

(　　)

(2) ア<u>The</u> mail had イ<u>already</u> been ウ<u>delivering</u> by the time I left エ<u>for school</u> this morning.

[創価大]

(　　)

(3) I ア<u>was</u> イ<u>pleasant</u> to hear ウ<u>about</u> エ<u>the birth</u> of your son.

[愛知学院大]

(　　)

(4) ア<u>I surprised to know</u> the actual conditions イ<u>that homeless people face</u> ウ<u>in their daily life</u>.

[上智大]

(　　)

08 | 比　較

🖐 要点整理

❶ 同じ意味を表す様々な比較表現

> Bob is **the tallest** boy in our class.

= Bob is **taller than any other** boy in our class.

= **No (other)** boy in our class is **taller than**〔**as tall as**〕Bob.

❷ 比較に関する注意すべき表現

(1) 原　級

> This country is **twice as** large **as** Japan.

> He is **not so much** an acquaintance **as** a friend.

= He is a friend **rather than** an acquaintance.（～よりはむしろ…）

> He did**n't so much as** ask me to sit down.（～すらしない）

(2) 比較級

> You can **no more** trust him **than** a hen can trust a fox.

（めんどりが狐を信用できないのと同様に君は彼を信用できない。）

no more than = only, **no less than** = as many〔much〕as

not more than = at most, **not less than** = at least

(3) 最上級

> The cherry blossoms will be **at their best** next week.

> You should **make the most of** your time.（～を最大限に活用する）

to the best of one's knowledge = *as far as* one knows

not ～ in the least（少しも～ではない）

❸ than を用いない比較級

be junior *to* ～「～より若い」，be senior *to* ～「～より年上である」，be superior *to* ～「～より優れている」，be inferior *to* ～「～より劣っている」

---

1 次の各文の（　）内に下から適当なものを選び，記号で答えよ。

(1) Generally, professional soccer players earn（　　　　）money than professional baseball players in Japan.

［亜細亜大］

ア fewer　　　イ little　　　ウ less　　　エ few

(2) Your bag is（　　　）heavier than it looks.

［京都産業大］

ア a lot　　　イ far too　　　ウ much more　　　エ so

(3) This is the third (　　　) city in Japan. 　　　[松山大]

ア large 　　イ larger 　　ウ largest 　　エ more large

(4) My father is (　　　) of the two men standing at the gate. 　　　[近畿大]

ア more tall 　　イ taller 　　ウ the tall 　　エ the taller

(5) When I take a trip to Tokyo, I (　　　) flying to going by train. 　　　[大阪学院大]

ア prefer 　　イ choose 　　ウ like 　　エ enjoy

(6) Emily is (　　　) than beautiful.

ア cute 　　イ cuter 　　ウ more cute 　　エ most cute

(7) My father is (　　　) than my mother. 　　　[桜美林大]

ア older three 　　　　　　イ three years older

ウ by three years old 　　　エ older to three years

(8) Jane picked up (　　　) tomatoes in the garden as Lisa did. 　　　[近畿大]

ア as twice many 　　イ so many twice 　　ウ twice as many 　　エ twice so many

(9) That player is not so (　　　) a genius as a hard worker. 　　　[中京大]

ア much 　　イ little 　　ウ more 　　エ less

(10) We invited ten guests, but there were (　　　) seven chairs.

ア no more than 　　　イ no less than

ウ not less than 　　　エ as many as

☆ **2** 次の各組の英文がほぼ同じ内容になるように，＿＿＿に適当な語を入れよ。

[大阪大谷大-改]

(1) { This river is the longest in the world.
　　＿＿＿＿＿＿ other river in the world is as long as this river.

[昭和女子大]

(2) { He is too wise to do such a foolish thing.
　　He knows ＿＿＿＿＿ ＿＿＿＿＿ to do such a foolish thing.

[駒澤大]

(3) { She is just as lovely as her sister.
　　She is no ＿＿＿＿＿ lovely than her sister.

[昭和女子大]

(4) { This bridge is twice the length of that one.
　　This bridge is ＿＿＿＿＿ ＿＿＿＿＿ long ＿＿＿＿＿ that one.

[大阪大谷大]

(5) { His plan is better than ours.
　　His plan is superior ＿＿＿＿＿ ours.

[獨協大]

(6) { Time is the most precious thing.
　　Time is more precious than ＿＿＿＿＿ ＿＿＿＿＿.

25

09 | 関係詞

🖐 要点整理

❶ 関係詞の注意すべき用法

(1) **that** は先行詞が「人」と「物」の両方に用いられるが，ⓐ先行詞が，「**人と物**」の場合や，ⓑ **強調**の語を伴う先行詞の場合は that が用いられる。

ⓐ Here come *the man and his dog* **that** have won the first prize.

ⓑ This is *the best* cake **that** I've ever eaten.

(2) 関係代名詞 **that** は前置詞の直後に置くことはできない。

> Is this the man ~~of that~~ you were talking ?　　　　　（誤）

> Is this the man **of whom** you were talking ?　　　　　（正）

> Is this the man (**whom**〔that〕) you were talking **of** ?　（正）

(3) 先行詞が「物」であっても，**that** は継続用法に用いることはできない。

> Smoking, **which**〔*that*〕is a bad habit, is still popular.

(4) **前文の内容，またはその一部を受ける**ことのできる関係代名詞は **which** である。

> He *broke his promise*, **which** made me angry.

（彼は約束を破った。それが私を怒らせたのだ。）

❷ what の慣用表現

> The old man is **what is called** a mine of information.（いわゆる）

> Legs **are to** the bike **what** an engine **is to** the car.

（脚と自転車との関係は，エンジンと車の関係と同じです。）

what is ＋比較級「さらに～なことに」　**what is better**〔**worse**〕

❸ 特殊な関係詞 … such~ as … / the same~ as … / but

> Let children read **such** books **as** will help them.

> There is no rule **but** has（= *that* doesn*'t* have）some exceptions.

（例外のない規則はない。）

❹ 複合関係詞 … who(m)ever, whichever, whatever など

> **Whoever**（= *No matter who*）may say so, I'll not believe him.〔副詞節〕

> You may take **whatever**（= *anything that*）you like.〔名詞節〕

❺ 関係副詞　接続詞と副詞の働きを兼ねるものである。

> Sunday is the day **when**（= *on which*）I am least busy.

> Do you remember the hotel **where**（= *at which*）we stayed ?

> Please give me a reason **why**（= *for which*）you made that mistake.

> This is $\begin{cases} \textbf{how} \\ \textbf{the way}(\textit{in which}) \end{cases}$ it happened. （こうしてそれは起こった。）
〔how と the way は同時には用いられない。〕

1 次の各文の＿＿に適当な関係詞を入れよ。

(1) The time has come ＿＿＿＿＿ we can travel to the moon. ［大阪産業大］

☆ (2) There is no one in the world ＿＿＿＿＿ sometimes commits errors.

(3) Reading is to the mind ＿＿＿＿＿ food is to the body. ［東京理科大］

(4) This is the restaurant ＿＿＿＿＿ he used to have lunch.

(5) It's snowing — that's ＿＿＿＿＿ I didn't come by car.

☆ (6) ＿＿＿＿＿ is done cannot be undone.

(7) He always comes home after midnight, and ＿＿＿＿＿ is more, he is drunk.

☆ (8) She expects me to clean the house in half an hour, ＿＿＿＿＿ is impossible.

(9) We often go shopping with Mr. and Mrs. Brown, both of ＿＿＿＿＿ are very kind.

☆ (10) In those days I believed everything ＿＿＿＿＿ my parents told me.

☆ **2** 次の各文の＿＿に下から適当なものを選んで入れよ。ただし，同じ語を２度使わないこと。

(1) Here are two books — take ＿＿＿＿＿ you like.

(2) Come ＿＿＿＿＿ it is convenient for you.

(3) ＿＿＿＿＿ wants to come to the party is welcome.

(4) He tells the same story to ＿＿＿＿＿ he meets.

(5) I will drive you ＿＿＿＿＿ you want to go.

(6) You can do ＿＿＿＿＿ you like.

〔whoever, whomever, whatever, whenever, wherever, whichever〕

advice
1 (2)「時々誤りを犯すということのない人は，この世には一人もいない」の意味。
(8)前文の内容，またはその一部を受ける関係代名詞。

3 次の各文の下線部の誤りを正せ。

☆ (1) Her hat, <u>that</u> is blue, goes well with her hair.

_____

(2) This is the same man <u>what</u> I saw in the train.

[広島経済大-改]

_____

(3) She tells that story to <u>whomever</u> will listen.

_____

(4) The house <u>which</u> Washington was born is open to the public.

_____

☆ (5) Rats were running about the attic all night, <u>that</u> kept us awake.

_____

☆ (6) The man to <u>that</u> you spoke the other day is my uncle.

_____

4 次の各文の( )内に下から適当なものを選び，記号で答えよ。

(1) It doesn't matter whether you win or lose the race. (　　) you have to do is try your best.　　　　　　　　　　　　　　　　　　　　　　　　　　　　[九州産業大]

　　ア All　　　イ Only　　　ウ That　　　エ Thing　　　オ Which

(2) We gave the road map to (　　) was not familiar with the country.　　[共立女子大]

　　ア wherever　　イ whichever　　ウ whoever　　エ whomever

(3) My mother may have to go into hospital, in (　　) case she won't be going on holiday.

　　ア such a　　イ its　　ウ which　　エ whose

(4) (　　) with singing and joking, the time passed quickly.

　　ア Which　　イ What　　ウ When　　エ Where

(5) Mr.Morris is now teaching at Central High School, (　　) is close to the Palace.

[京都学園大]

　　ア what　　イ which　　ウ who　　エ where

---

advice

3 (3) whomever は will listen の主語として不適当。
4 (4) what with A and B「AやらBやらで」の意味の慣用句。

5 次の各文の下線部のうち，文法的に誤りのあるものを１つ選び，記号で答えよ。

(1) ア<u>Most of you</u> イ<u>can probably think of</u> ウ<u>a dozen countries</u> エ<u>that you would like to go.</u>

［法政大］

(　　　)

(2) ア<u>All things considered,</u> イ<u>spring</u> is the season ウ<u>when</u> I like エ<u>best.</u>　　　　［福島大］

(　　　)

(3) The high school girl ア<u>whose</u> bicycle イ<u>was stolen</u> ウ<u>who</u> reported its loss エ<u>to</u> the police.

［明海大］

(　　　)

(4) The man ア<u>whom</u> I thought was イ<u>a friend</u> ウ<u>suddenly</u> grabbed me エ<u>by the arm</u> and took me away.　　　　　　　　　　　　　　　　　　　　　　　　　　　　［専修大］

(　　　)

(5) ア<u>If you cannot find</u> イ<u>that</u> you are ウ<u>looking for,</u> please エ<u>ask us</u> at the information desk.

［東京都市大］

(　　　)

(6) ア<u>Whatever</u> you have questions, please イ<u>feel</u> free to ウ<u>go</u> and エ<u>talk to</u> your professor.

［南山大］

(　　　)

(7) My ア<u>wonderful</u> teachers from Italy, neither of イ<u>who</u> you have ウ<u>ever</u> had the pleasure of エ<u>meeting,</u> will be arriving here shortly.　　　　　　　　　　　　　　［神奈川大］

(　　　)

(8) When I met her for the first time ア<u>in twenty years,</u> I found that she was イ<u>no longer</u> ウ<u>that</u> she エ<u>used to be.</u>　　　　　　　　　　　　　　　　　　　　　　　　［東海大］

(　　　)

(9) ア<u>What</u> イ<u>confused</u> me was ウ<u>what</u> Kate エ<u>kept</u> silent.　　　　［大阪経済大-改］

(　　　)

(10) ア<u>The cost</u> of a barrel of oil イ<u>is</u> almost double ウ<u>which</u> it エ<u>was</u> last year.

［武庫川女子大-改］

(　　　)

(11) ア<u>I have</u> a dog, イ<u>that</u> I got ウ<u>from</u> my エ<u>neighbor.</u>

(　　　)

10 | 仮定法

月　　日

解答 ▶ 別冊p.7

要点整理

❶ 仮定法過去

If ＋ S' ＋動詞の過去形 ..., S ＋ would〔could など〕＋動詞の原形 ～.

現在の事実に反する仮定を表す。

> **If I knew** his telephone number, I **could call** him up.
>   = As I don't know his telephone number, I can't call him up.

❷ 仮定法過去完了

If ＋ S' ＋ had ＋動詞の過去分詞 ..., S ＋ would〔could など〕have ＋動詞の過去分詞 ～.

過去の事実に反する仮定を表す。

> **If** you **had been** at the meeting, **I could have seen** you.
>   = As you weren't at the meeting, I couldn't see you.

❸ 注意すべき仮定法の表現

> **If** anyone **should** call on me, please take a message.〔実現の可能性が少ない仮定〕

> **I wish** I **could** speak English. = I am sorry I can't speak English.

> **If it were not for** your advice, I **would** fail.（～がなければ）
>   = **But for**〔**Without**〕your advice, I **would** fail.

> They treat me **as if I were** their own son.（まるで～かのように）

> **Were** you to try harder, I'm sure you **would** succeed.〔省略による倒置〕
>   = **If** you **were** to try harder, I'm sure you **would** succeed.

> I suggested that she (**should**) **go** by herself.

〔仮定法現在：命令・提案を表す that 節内〕

☆ **1** 次の各文の（　）内に下から適当なものを選び，記号で答えよ。

(1) If I were you, I (　　　) him. 〔流通経済大〕

　ア help　　　　　**イ** helped　　　　**ウ** had helped　　　　**エ** would help

(2) (　　　) a severe earthquake happen, what would you do ? 〔青山学院大〕

　ア If it were for　　**イ** Could　　**ウ** Should　　**エ** What if

(3) If she had taken the first train, she (　　　) here now. 〔東京電機大〕

　ア was　　　　　　**イ** would be

　ウ had been　　　　**エ** would have been

(4) "There was a good soccer match last week." [摂南大]
"If I had known about it, I (　　　) a ticket."
ア would buy　　　　　　　　イ should buy
ウ could buy　　　　　　　　エ would have bought

(5) (　　　) the doctor's quick treatment at that time, I would not be alive now. [昭和女子大]
ア If it had not been for　　　イ If it were not for
ウ If there were not　　　　　エ If I did not receive

(6) (　　　) William, we would never have found the way. [徳島文理大]
ア But　　　　　イ Without　　　　ウ Except　　　　エ Within

(7) She can speak English well (　　　) it were her mother tongue. [千葉工業大]
ア as if　　　　　イ if　　　　　ウ unless　　　　エ even if

(8) Nancy insisted that she (　　　) to the farewell party. [西南学院大]
ア be invited　　　イ being invited　　　ウ would invite　　　エ is going to invite

2 次の各組の英文がほぼ同じ内容になるように，＿＿＿に適当な語を入れよ。

☆ (1) ⎰ He recommended me, so I got a promotion. [昭和女子大]
　　 ⎱ ＿＿＿＿＿ ＿＿＿＿＿ his recommendation, I would not have got a promotion.

(2) ⎰ If the driver had been a little more careful, he could have avoided such a tragic accident. [(2)・(3)広島修道大]
　 ⎱ ＿＿＿＿＿ a little more care, the driver could have avoided such a tragic accident.

(3) ⎰ A step forward, and you would have fallen over the cliff.
　 ⎱ If you ＿＿＿＿＿ ＿＿＿＿＿ a step forward, you would have fallen over the cliff.

(4) ⎰ I am disappointed that he is not here. [玉川大]
　 ⎱ ＿＿＿＿＿ only he were here!

☆ (5) ⎰ Without his wife's money, he would never be a director.
　　 ⎱ Were ＿＿＿＿＿ not for his wife's money, he would never be a director.

☆ (6) ⎰ I'm sorry I can't help you. [神戸松蔭女子学院大]
　　 ⎱ I ＿＿＿＿＿ I ＿＿＿＿＿ help you.

11 | 話法・時制の一致

要点整理

❶ **話法を転換** … 伝達動詞，時制，代名詞，副詞などに注意

　ⓐ直接話法，ⓑ間接話法

> ⓐ They **said to** me, "**We have** not heard anything about it." 〔平叙文〕
  = ⓑ They **told** me (that) **they had** not heard anything about it.

> ⓐ Father **said to** me, "Who **is** going to cook lunch **today**?" 〔Wh- 疑問文〕
  = ⓑ Father **asked** me who **was** going to cook lunch **that day**.

> ⓐ He **said to** me, "**Did you hear** her go out?" 〔Yes-No 疑問文〕
  = ⓑ He **asked** me **if I had heard** her go out.

> ⓐ I **said to** her, "**Take** a look at **yourself** in the mirror." 〔命令文〕
  = ⓑ I **told** her **to take** a look at **herself** in the mirror.

> ⓐ She **said to** him, "**Don't** leave the door open, please." 〔否定の命令文〕
  = ⓑ She **asked** him **not to** leave the door open.

> ⓐ She **said**, "**How** beautiful the sunset **is**!" 〔感嘆文〕
  = ⓑ She **exclaimed** that the sunset **was very** beautiful.

❷ **時制の一致の例外** … 不変の真理，現在の習慣，歴史的過去，仮定法

> We *learned* that the Second World War **broke** (had broken) out in 1939.

> He *said to* me, "What **would** you do if you **were** in my place?"
  = He *asked* me what I **would** do if I **were** in his place.

☆ **1** 次の各組の英文がほぼ同じ内容になるように，＿＿に適当な語を入れよ。

(1) { He said to me, "It's very kind of you to invite me to the party."
　　 He ＿＿＿＿＿ me that it ＿＿＿＿＿ very kind of ＿＿＿＿＿ to invite ＿＿＿＿＿ to the party.

(2) { I said to him, "What are you doing?"
　　 I ＿＿＿＿＿ him what ＿＿＿＿＿ ＿＿＿＿＿ doing.

(3) { He said, "I bought this watch last year."
　　 He said that ＿＿＿＿＿ ＿＿＿＿＿ ＿＿＿＿＿ ＿＿＿＿＿ watch the year ＿＿＿＿＿.

(4) { Mother said to me, "Please don't forget to post the letter."
　　 Mother ＿＿＿＿＿ me ＿＿＿＿＿ ＿＿＿＿＿ ＿＿＿＿＿ to post the letter.

(5) { He said, "Let's go for a drive."
　　 He ＿＿＿＿＿ that ＿＿＿＿＿ ＿＿＿＿＿ go for a drive.

2 次の各文の____に適当な語を入れ，直接話法の文を完成させよ。

(1) Mother told me to wait till she returned.

= Mother _____ to me, "_____ till _____ _____."

(2) I asked her if she had ever been to Paris.

= I _____ to her, "_____ _____ ever been to Paris ?"

(3) He told me that I had better stay there till the following day.

= He said to me, "_____ _____ better stay_____ till _____."

(4) Jack suggested that we should play tennis the next day.

= Jack _____, "_____ play tennis _____."

(5) He asked the boys who they thought she was.

= He said to the boys, "_____ _____ _____ _____ she

_____ ?"

☆ **3** 次の各文の（　）内の動詞を最も適当な時制にせよ。

(1) All the students knew that the earth (go) round the sun.

_____

(2) I learned that World War II (end) in 1945.

_____

(3) It was colder yesterday than it (be) today.

_____

(4) He told me that if he (be) younger, he would try it again.

_____

4 日本語を参考に，（　）内の語句を並べかえよ。

(1) 母はいつも私に，寝不足だと勉強に身が入らないよ，と言っています。　　　　　［桜美林大］

Mother always (that if / I don't sleep well / on my studies / tells me / I can't focus / ,).

Mother always _____

_____.

(2) 食堂まで歩きたくなければ家に配達してくれる「出前」があるかどうか聞いてごらんなさい。

［拓殖大］

If you don't (a restaurant / ask if / "demae" which / feel like / means home / they have

/ walking to / ,) delivery system.

If you don't _____

_____ delivery system.

12 否 定

🖑 要点整理

❶ 準否定語

> I **hardly** 〔**scarcely**〕 remember what I said. (ほとんど～ない)

> She **seldom** speaks ill of others. (めったに～ない)

❷ ⓐ部分否定とⓑ全否定

- ⓐ **Not all** the students *are* present. (すべてが～するわけではない)
- ⓑ **None** of the students *are* present. (だれも～しない)
- ⓐ I do**n't** know **both** of them. (両方とも～わけではない)
- ⓑ I know **neither** of them. (両方とも～ない)
- ⓐ I'm **not always** at home on Sunday. (いつも～とは限らない)
- ⓑ I'm **never** at home on Sunday. (決して～しない)

❸ 慣用表現

never ... without ～ing 「～することなしに決して…しない，…すると必ず～する」，

anything but ～ = far from ～ 「決して～ではない」，

the last person to ～ 「決して～する人ではない」

☆ **1** 次の各文の（　）内に下から適当なものを選び，記号で答えよ。

(1) These people are far（　　　）innocent.　　　　　　　　　　　　　　　　　　　[金城学院大]

　　ア from　　　　　**イ** in　　　　**ウ** of　　　　**エ** on

(2) I（　　　）ever go on a trip alone. I like company.　　　　　　　　　　　　　[日本大]

　　ア almost　　　　**イ** hardly　　　　**ウ** nearly　　　　**エ** always

(3) *A :* Do you mind if I smoke here ?　　　　　　　　　　　　　　　　　　　　　[九州産業大－改]

　　B :（　　　）. I strongly dislike cigarette smoke.

　　ア Certainly not　　　　**イ** Go ahead　　　　**ウ** I'd rather you didn't

(4) *A :* Can you lend me a few dollars ?

　　B :（　　　）.

　　ア I'm afraid not　　　　**イ** I hope not　　　　**ウ** I think not

(5) We（　　　）be too careful in climbing a mountain in winter.

　　ア ought to　　　　**イ** must not　　　　**ウ** cannot　　　　**エ** need not

2 次の各組の英文がほぼ同じ内容になるように，＿＿＿に適当な語を入れよ。

☆ (1)
{ I'm absolutely sure that he'll never do such a thing.
{ He'll be the ＿＿＿＿＿ person to do such a thing.

[学習院大]

(2)
{ I advise you to see a lawyer.
{ Why ＿＿＿＿＿ you see a lawyer ?

[関西学院大]

(3)
{ He talks very little.
{ He is a man of ＿＿＿＿＿ words.

[専修大]

☆ (4)
{ His manners are far from pleasant.
{ His manners are ＿＿＿＿＿ but pleasant.

[大東文化大]

(5)
{ Who can trust such a dishonest politician ?
{ ＿＿＿＿＿ can trust such a dishonest politician.

[大東文化大]

☆ (6)
{ Whenever we meet, we have a quarrel.
{ We never meet ＿＿＿＿＿ ＿＿＿＿＿.

[神戸松蔭女子学院大]

☆ (7)
{ I have no connection with the matter at all.
{ I have ＿＿＿＿＿ to do with the matter at all.

[大阪大谷大]

(8)
{ Nobody is more eloquent than he in the world of politics.
{ He is second to ＿＿＿＿＿ in eloquence in the world of politics.

[広島修道大]

3 日本語を参考に，＿＿＿に適当な語を入れよ。

(1) 彼らはみんなすっかり疲れてしまって，ただあくびしか出なかった。

They were all so tired they could do ＿＿＿＿＿ ＿＿＿＿＿ yawn.

[立命館大]

(2) これはあなたには全く関係がないことだ。

This is ＿＿＿＿＿ of your business.

[学習院大]

(3) ときどきスポーツをすることは決して時間の浪費ではない。

Playing sports from time to time is by ＿＿＿＿＿ ＿＿＿＿＿ a waste of time.

[立命館大]

(4) 彼はスポーツが好きじゃない。ぼくも好きじゃない。

He is not fond of sports, and I am not ＿＿＿＿＿.

[学習院大]

advice -
2 (6) never ... without ～ing 「～することなしに…しない」の二重否定。

13 ｜ 無生物主語・名詞構文

要点整理

❶ 無生物主語によく用いられる動詞

> *This medicine* will **make** you feel better.

> *A traffic accident* **caused** him to be late for school.

> *Airplanes* **enable** us to go around the world in a few days.

> *The heavy rain* **compelled** us to put off our departure.

> *This bus* will **take** you to the museum.

> *Today's paper* **says** that a big typhoon is approaching.

> *The cold weather* **prevented** us from going out.

> *This picture* always **reminds** me of my hometown.

> *Her pride* did not **allow** her to do such a mean thing.

　これらの文を，人間を主語にして書き換えると，無生物主語の部分は節や句になることが多い。例えば最後の文は次のようになる。

> *She* couldn't do such a mean thing **because she was so *proud*.**

❷ 動詞を名詞で表現する。

> I am sure **that she will *marry*.**

= I am sure **of her *marriage*.**

> Please let me know **when you will *arrive*.**

= Please let me know **the time of your *arrival*.**

☆ **1** 次の各組の英文がほぼ同じ内容になるように，＿＿に適当な語を入れよ。

(1) ⎰ If you take a little walk, you will have a good appetite.　　　　　　［昭和女子大］
　　⎱ A little walk will ＿＿＿＿＿＿ ＿＿＿＿＿＿ a good appetite.

(2) ⎰ I am sure that he will succeed.　　　　　　　　　　　　　　　　　　［工学院大］
　　⎱ I am sure ＿＿＿＿＿＿ his ＿＿＿＿＿＿.

(3) ⎰ Being a proud person, she could not apologize to him frankly.　　　　［大東文化大］
　　⎱ Her ＿＿＿＿＿＿ did not allow ＿＿＿＿＿＿ to apologize to him frankly.

(4) ⎰ There is no hope of his recovery.　　　　　　　　　　　　　　　　　［大阪大谷大］
　　⎱ There is no hope that ＿＿＿＿＿＿ ＿＿＿＿＿＿ ＿＿＿＿＿＿.

(5) ⎰ If you walk about five minutes, you will get to the lake.　　　　　　［梅光女学院大］
　　⎱ About five ＿＿＿＿＿＿ ＿＿＿＿＿＿ will take you to the lake.

(6) $\left\{\begin{array}{l}\text{We could not go to the mountains, because it rained.} \\ \text{Rain \underline{\hspace{2cm}} us \underline{\hspace{2cm}} \underline{\hspace{2cm}} to the mountains.}\end{array}\right.$ [工学院大]

(7) $\left\{\begin{array}{l}\text{How did you come to this conclusion ?} \\ \text{\underline{\hspace{2cm}} led you to this conclusion ?}\end{array}\right.$ [亜細亜大]

(8) $\left\{\begin{array}{l}\text{What has disappointed you ?} \\ \text{\underline{\hspace{2cm}} are you disappointed ?}\end{array}\right.$ [工学院大]

2 次の各文を指示に従って書きかえよ。

(1) Because of her illness, she was compelled to stop studying.

(Her illness を主語にして，かつ to 不定詞を用いて) [名城大]

_____

(2) I was astonished <u>that he had succeeded</u>. (下線部を副詞句に書き換えて) [工学院大]

_____

(3) We could not go on a picnic because of rain last Sunday. (Rain を主語にして) [鹿児島大]

_____

(4) If you go along this road, you will get to the station. (This road を主語にして) [工学院大]

_____

3 日本語を参考に，（　）内の語句を並べかえよ。

(1) その映画は昔の日本の様子を見せてくれる。 [東京理科大]

The film (be / how / Japan / like / shows / to / used / what). 〔1 語不要〕

The film _____ .

(2) この薬を飲めばよくなると思いますよ。 [中京大]

I think that this (make / will / better / medicine / feel / you).

I think that this _____ .

(3) 驚きのあまり言葉にならなかった。 [九州国際大]

(astonishment / power / my / of / me / deprived) of speech.

_____ of speech.

(4) 毎日うがいをすると風邪をひきません。 [中部大]

(catching / colds / day / every / from / gargling / keep / will / you).

_____ .

🖑 要点整理

❶ 主語と動詞の呼応 … 呼応

(1) not only A but (also) B，B as well as A，either A or B，neither A nor B が主語のとき，**動詞は B の人称・数に呼応**する。

> **I** as well as you **am** to blame for the accident.

(2) 不定代名詞 each，either，neither，学問名(*e.g.* physics)，1 組の名詞(*e.g.* bread and butter)などは**単数**扱い。

> **Each** of the girls was dressed in beautiful silk.

❷ 否定語を文頭に出すと，その後の語順は疑問文と同じ語順になる。 … 倒置

> ***Little*** **did I** dream that I would lose my job.
> "I haven't seen the movie." "***Neither*** **have I**."

❸ 強調構文 … 強調

> *You* are in the wrong. → **It's** *you* **that** are in the wrong.

❹ 助動詞 do，did による強調 … 強調

> He said that he would come, and he **did** *come*.

❺ 語句の繰り返しを避ける。 … 省略

> Jane is *a good pianist*, as her mother used to be (*a good pianist*).

❻ 慣用表現 … 省略

if any「もしあれば」，if possible「もし可能なら」

---

1 次の各文の(　)内に下から適当なものを選び，記号で答えよ。

☆ (1) Where do you suppose (　　　) yesterday ? [梅花女子大]

 ア did they go   **イ** had they gone
 ウ they have gone   **エ** they went

☆ (2) It was because he was ill (　　　) we decided to return. [関東学院大]

 ア that   **イ** for   **ウ** which   **エ** why

☆ (3) Little (　　　) that his son would behave so wildly. [龍谷大]

 ア did he dream   **イ** he dreamed
 ウ did he not dream **エ** he did not dream

☆ (4) "I've never visited this city before." "(   )."

    ア So do I   **イ** So did I

    ウ Neither have I   **エ** Neither did I

(5) Tom almost never studied while he was at college, (   )?   [日本大]

    ア didn't he   **イ** did he   **ウ** wasn't he   **エ** was he

2 次の各文の(　)内から適当なものを選べ。

(1) Neither Mildred nor her friend (wants,　want) to spend the spring vacation at home.

                                         [(1)～(3)聖心女子大]

☆ (2) The number of books in the library (is,　are) large.

(3) The first two parts of the experiment (takes,　take) the most time.

                                       [(4)・(5)梅花女子大]

☆ (4) Each of them had to do (his,　our) best.

(5) Ten dollars (is,　are) too much for me to pay.

3 次の各文で省略できる語を，それぞれ**ア～オ**のうちから選び，記号で答えよ。

(1) The doctor ordered me that I should take no coffee.   (　　)
    ア   **イ** **ウ** **エ**   **オ**

(2) I had my hair cut at a barber's shop two weeks ago.   (　　)
   ア **イ**   **ウ**   **エ**   **オ**

(3) Reading magazines helps me to pass away on such a rainy day.   (　　)
        ア   **イ** **ウ**   **エ**   **オ**

(4) She gave so witty an answer that everyone burst out laughing.   (　　)
       ア   **イ**   **ウ**   **エ**   **オ**

☆ **4** 次の各組の英文がほぼ同じ内容になるように，＿＿に適当な語を入れよ。

(1)   He didn't arrive until the meal was over.
      It was ＿＿＿＿＿ ＿＿＿＿＿ the meal was over ＿＿＿＿＿ he ＿＿＿＿＿.

(2)   As soon as he went to bed, he fell asleep.
      ＿＿＿＿＿ sooner ＿＿＿＿＿ he gone to bed ＿＿＿＿＿ he fell asleep.

advice

2 (1) neither A nor B が主語の場合，動詞は B に呼応する。
    (5) Ten dollars を 1 つの単位として考える。

15 | 接続詞

要点整理

❶ 命令文 , and 〜 ; 命令文 , or 〜

> **Take** a taxi, **and** you will be in time for the train.（…せよ，そうすれば〜）

> **Hurry** up, **or** you will be late for class.（…せよ，さもないと〜）

❷ It is true (that) 〜, but ... = Indeed 〜, but ... … 「確かに〜だが…」

> **It is true** that he is clever, **but** he has no common sense.

❸ nor〔neither〕によって起こる倒置

> He doesn't like coffee, **nor**〔**neither**〕 do I.（私も嫌いだ）

❹ not only A but (also) B = B as well as A … 「AだけでなくBも」

> He is well-known **not only** in Japan **but** all over the world.

❺ unless = if not … 「もし〜でなければ」

> **Unless** you apologize at once, I will never speak to you again.

❻ It will not be long before 〜 … 「間もなく〜するだろう」

> **It will not be long before** he arrives here.

❼ The moment〔instant，minute〕〜 = As soon as 〜 … 「〜するとすぐに」

> **As soon as** he started, it began to rain.

>   = **No sooner** had he started **than** it began to rain.

>   = **Hardly**〔**Scarcely**〕 had he started **when**〔**before**〕 it began to rain.

❽ lest 〜 (should)動詞の原形 = for fear (that) 〜 should ... … 「〜が…しないように」

> He takes care **lest** he catch cold.

>   = He takes care **for fear** he **should** catch cold.

---

1 次の各文の（　）内に下から適当なものを選び，記号で答えよ。

(1) He studied fine art（　　　）he was in France.

　　ア during 　　　　　イ if 　　　　　　ウ while 　　　　　エ among

☆ (2)（　　　）you are a high-school girl, you ought to know better.

　　ア So that 　　　　イ Now that 　　　ウ After that 　　　エ In order that

☆ (3) We do not appreciate our health (　　　) we get sick.

　　　ア　though　　　　　イ　until　　　　　ウ　when　　　　　エ　because

(4) You can stay here (　　　) you are quiet.

　　　ア　but　　　　　イ　as far as　　　　ウ　as long as　　　　エ　whether

(5) You may come (　　　) it is convenient.　　　　　　　　　　　　　　　　[東洋大]

　　　ア　whenever　　　イ　whichever　　　ウ　whomever　　　エ　whatever

☆ (6) You won't catch the train (　　　) you hurry.

　　　ア　and　　　　　イ　as　　　　　ウ　lest　　　　　エ　unless

(7) You must leave now; (　　　), you will be late for your social studies class.　[センター試験]

　　　ア　instead　　　イ　therefore　　　ウ　otherwise　　　エ　accordingly

2 次の各組の英文がほぼ同じ内容になるように，＿＿に適当な語を入れよ。

(1) ⎰ In spite of his hard work, he was deeply in debt.　　　　　　　　[駒澤大]
　　⎱ ＿＿＿＿＿＿＿ he worked hard, he was deeply in debt.

☆ (2) ⎰ She stepped aside to let me pass.
　　　 ⎱ She stepped aside ＿＿＿＿＿＿ that I could pass.

☆ (3) ⎰ If you sit back and rest, you will feel much better.
　　　 ⎱ Sit back and rest, ＿＿＿＿＿＿ you will feel much better.

(4) ⎰ Do you mind my using this telephone ?
　　⎱ Do you mind ＿＿＿＿＿＿ I use this telephone ?

　　　　　　　　　　　　　　　　　　　　　　　　　　　　　　　　　[広島修道大]
☆ (5) ⎰ The baby stopped crying only when he was fed.
　　　 ⎱ It was not ＿＿＿＿＿＿ the baby was fed that he stopped crying.

3 次の各組の英文の＿＿に共通して入る語を書け。

(1) ⎰ We see things differently according ＿＿＿＿＿＿ we are rich or poor.
　　⎱ He came late, ＿＿＿＿＿＿ is often the case with him.

☆ (2) ⎰ I'll be back in a ＿＿＿＿＿＿. (m で始まる語)
　　　 ⎱ He ran away the ＿＿＿＿＿＿ he saw me.

(3) ⎰ This machine is out of ＿＿＿＿＿＿. (o で始まる語)
　　⎱ He works hard in ＿＿＿＿＿＿ that his family may be happy.

advice ┄┄┄

2 (5) The baby didn't stop crying until he was fed. を強調構文にすると？

16 | 名詞・冠詞

要点整理

❶ 注意すべき集合名詞 … 名詞

> There *was* **a large audience** in the stadium.〔単数〕
> **The audience** *were* all excited.〔複数〕
> **The police** *are* looking into the matter.〔常に複数〕

❷ 注意すべき抽象名詞 … 名詞

> of importance（= important），with ease（= easily）

❸ 注意すべき不可算名詞 … 名詞

luggage（（英））= baggage（（米）），furniture，advice，information，news などは
(a) little，a lot of，a piece of などと用いる。これらの名詞は複数形不可。

❹ the ＋形容詞 / 分詞「〜な人々」 … 冠詞

> **The rich**（= Rich people）are not always happy.

❺ 冠詞の注意すべき位置 … 冠詞

> in **such *a* short** time = in **so short *a*** time

❻ 身体の一部を指す表現 … 冠詞

> My teacher patted *me* **on the head**.〔patted my head より一般的〕

---

１ 次の各文の（　）内に下から適当なものを選び，記号で答えよ。

☆ (1) It was (　　　　) that we decided to go on a picnic.
　　ア on a such fine day　　　　**イ** on so a fine day
　　ウ on such a fine day　　　　**エ** on such fine a day

☆ (2) He will feed (　　　　).
　　ア hungry　　　**イ** a hungry　　　**ウ** hunger　　　**エ** the hungry

☆ (3) We don't have (　　　　) snow this year.　　　　　　　　〔三重中京大〕
　　ア many　　　**イ** few　　　**ウ** much

(4) My sister is in her (　　　　).　　　　　　　　　　　　　〔学習院大〕
　　ア twenties　　**イ** twentieth　　**ウ** twenty　　**エ** twenty-year-old

(5) Please hold the (　　　　) for a moment.　He's on another phone.　［青山学院大-改］
　ア conversation　　　　イ call　　　　ウ line　　　　エ receiver

(6) My secretary has a good (　　　　) of English.　［名城大］
　ア interest　　　　イ speaker　　　　ウ command　　　　エ gift

☆ (7) I've got a dental (　　　　) at three o'clock.
　ア plan　　　　イ step　　　　ウ promise　　　　エ appointment

(8) The play was not a bit interesting, but there was (　　　　) in the theater.　［早稲田大］
　ア many audience　　　　イ a large audience　　　　ウ a lot more audience

(9) The Star Supermarket was very successful this year because it was so popular among its (　　　　).
　ア guests　　　　イ customers　　　　ウ audience　　　　エ visitors

☆ (10) However (　　　　) we gave him, he still does exactly what he wants to.
　ア lots of advice　　　　イ much advice
　ウ lot of advices　　　　エ many of advices

2 次の各文の下線部のうち，文法的に誤りのあるものを１つ選び，記号で答えよ。

(1) David bought a watch, but it ア<u>lost</u> two イ<u>minutes</u> ウ<u>a day</u>, so he returned エ<u>a watch</u>.　(　　　)

(2) It is ア<u>of no</u> イ<u>important</u> to ウ<u>discuss</u> エ<u>such</u> a little thing.　(　　　)

(3) All ア<u>informations</u> イ<u>can be</u> ウ<u>made</u> エ<u>bad use of</u>.　(　　　)

(4) I ア<u>tried to catch</u> イ<u>him</u> ウ<u>by</u> エ<u>his hand</u> but I couldn't.　(　　　)

(5) ア<u>How much</u> イ<u>does it cost</u> ウ<u>to send this parcel</u> エ<u>by the air</u> ?　(　　　)

(6) ア<u>The man</u> イ<u>got tired</u> ウ<u>after moving</u> エ<u>all the furnitures</u>.　(　　　)

(7) His work ア<u>isn't bad</u> but there イ<u>is</u> ウ<u>plenty of</u> エ<u>rooms</u> for improvement.　(　　　)

(8) We ア<u>had to</u> イ<u>make our way</u> ウ<u>with difficult</u> エ<u>up the mountain</u>.　［梅花女子大-改］
　(　　　)

----

advice
1 (6) command の基本の意味は「支配力，統率力」　(8) audience「聴衆」は population「人口」と同様 many などで修飾しない。　(10) advice は不可算名詞。
2 (2) of＋抽象名詞→形容詞　(8) with＋抽象名詞→副詞　*e.g.* with care → carefully

要点整理

❶ 再帰代名詞の注意すべき表現

> I **enjoyed myself** at the party last night.

> He **hurt himself** while skiing. = He was hurt while skiing.

> Please **help yourself to** some salad.（自分で取って食べる）

❷ it の用法

> **It** has been *raining* on and off since this morning.〔天候〕

> **It** took me three hours *to finish* this work.〔形式主語〕

> I think **it** impossible *to swim* across the river.〔形式目的語〕

> **It** was in 1939 *that* the Second World War broke out.〔強調構文〕

❸ 指示代名詞の注意すべき表現

> The climate here is like **that** (= the climate) of Japan.

> **Those** (who were) present all agreed to his proposal.（～する人々）

> He is captain and should be treated as **such**.
> （彼は主将であるので，それなりに扱われるべきだ。）

❹ 不定代名詞の注意すべき表現

> Replace the old tire with a new **one** (= tire).

> I don't like this dress; show me **another** (= another dress).

> To know is one thing, and to teach quite **another**.

> He has two daughters; one is in Tokyo, **the other** in Osaka.

---

1 次の各文の（　）内に下から適当なものを選び，記号で答えよ。

(1) "Did you all enjoy (　　　　)?" "Yes, we had a very good time."

　　ア myself　　　　イ yourself　　　　ウ ourselves　　　　エ yourselves

(2) "Have you got any money ?" "Yes, some but not (　　　　)."　　　　　　［日本大］

　　ア a few　　　　イ much　　　　ウ many　　　　エ few

(3) Heaven helps (　　　) who help themselves.

    ア one   **イ** that   **ウ** those   **エ** them

(4) The population of Tokyo is larger than (　　　) of Paris.

    ア one   **イ** that   **ウ** those   **エ** it

(5) (　　　) my friends live in Yokohama.　　　　　　　　　　　　　　[鶴見大]

    ア Almost of   **イ** Almost   **ウ** Most of   **エ** Most

(6) I am happiness (　　　).

    ア itself   **イ** myself   **ウ** oneself   **エ** self

(7) Ellen has three sisters. One is a student, and (　　　) are office workers.

    ア another   **イ** the other   **ウ** others   **エ** the others

(8) I found (　　　) difficult to solve the problem.

    ア it   **イ** this is   **ウ** that   **エ** that is

(9) I am a gentleman, and I will behave (　　　).

    ア as such   **イ** so like   **ウ** by it   **エ** for that

(10) Everybody's business is (　　　) business.　　　　　　　　　　　[桜美林大]

    ア nobody's   **イ** somebody's   **ウ** anybody's   **エ** Jack's

(11) Can you tell the difference between rice grown in Japan and (　　　)?　　[センター試験]

    ア American one   **イ** American rice

    ウ one grown in America   **エ** rice of America

---

2 次の各組の英文がほぼ同じ内容になるように，＿＿＿に適当な語を入れよ。

☆ (1) ｛ To earn and to save are two quite different things.　　　　　　[広島修道大]

      ｛ To earn is one thing; to save is quite ＿＿＿＿＿＿＿＿.

☆ (2) ｛ You have only to try hard.　　　　　　　　　　　　　　　　　[玉川大]

      ｛ ＿＿＿＿＿＿＿＿ you have to do is to try hard.

(3) ｛ It is no wonder that he failed.

    ｛ There is ＿＿＿＿＿＿＿＿ strange about his failure.

                                  [沖縄国際大-改]

(4) ｛ She is a vegetarian; she eats only vegetables.

    ｛ She is a vegetarian; she eats ＿＿＿＿＿＿＿＿ but vegetables.

☆ (5) ｛ We often hear people say that honesty is the best policy.

      ｛ We often hear ＿＿＿＿＿＿＿＿ said that honesty is the best policy.

👆 **要 点 整 理**

❶ **数量を表す形容詞** … 形容詞

(1) 「**数**」 (a) few，many，a great〔large，good〕number of

(2) 「**量**」 (a) little，much，a great〔good〕deal of

}，a lot of，plenty of

❷ **限定用法と叙述用法** … 形容詞

(1) **限定用法のみ**　mere，only，latter，elder，live[láiv] など。

(2) **叙述用法のみ**　asleep，awake，afraid，unable など。

❸ **混同しやすい形容詞** … 形容詞

{ imaginary 「想像上の」
　imaginable 「想像できる」
　imaginative 「想像力に富んだ」

{ sensitive 「敏感な」
　sensible 「分別のある」
　sensual 「官能的な」

❹ **限定用法と叙述用法では意味に違いのある形容詞** … 形容詞

> A **certain** salesman came to see me. （ある〜）

> It is **certain** that he will join us. （〜は確かだ）

❺ **混同しやすい副詞** … 副詞

> **late** 「遅く」，**lately** 「最近」，**near** 「近くに」，**nearly** 「ほとんど」

❻ **注意すべき enough の位置** … 副詞

副詞の enough は修飾する語の後ろに置く。

> I got up *early* **enough** to catch the first train.

❼ **very** … 副詞

形容詞・副詞の**原級**を修飾。また，**形容詞化した分詞**を修飾。

❽ **much** … 副詞

動詞，形容詞・副詞の**比較級**を修飾。また，**過去分詞**を修飾。

❾ **文副詞　文全体を修飾** … 副詞

> **Fortunately** the weather was fine.

　= It was fortunate that the weather was fine.

---

1 次の各文の（　）内に下から適当なものを選び，記号で答えよ。

☆ (1) (　　　　　) passengers in the bus were asleep when the accident happened.　　　［京都産業大］

　　ア Almost of　　　　　　　**イ** Almost of the

　　ウ Almost the　　　　　　　**エ** Almost all of the

(2) The coat is (　　　) big for me.　　　　　　　　　　　　　　[南山大]

　　ア much too　　　イ too much　　　ウ very much　　　エ much very

☆ (3) I'm afraid there isn't (　　　) coffee left.　　　　　　　　　[鶴見大]

　　ア any　　　イ some　　　ウ little　　　エ few

☆ (4) I'll be very (　　　) to see you again tomorrow.

　　ア pleasant　　　イ please　　　ウ pleased　　　エ pleasing

(5) I called him but the line was (　　　).　　　　　　　　　　　[朝日大]

　　ア over　　　イ up　　　ウ busy　　　エ tired

(6) I foolishly interpreted the idiom according to its (　　　) sense.　[梅花女子大]

　　ア literal　　　イ literally　　　ウ literary　　　エ literate

☆ (7) Milk is delivered (　　　) other day.　　　　　　　　　　[流通経済大]

　　ア every　　　イ all　　　ウ each　　　エ any

2 次の各文の(　)内の語を最も適当な形容詞または副詞にせよ。なお，変える必要のない語は，そのまま書くこと。

(1) The bed of the hotel room felt so (soft) for me that I couldn't sleep well.

＿＿＿＿＿＿＿＿＿

(2) The dragon is an (imagine) animal.

＿＿＿＿＿＿＿＿＿

(3) (Fortune) nobody was killed in the accident.

＿＿＿＿＿＿＿＿＿

3 次の各文の(　)内に下から適当なものを選び，記号で答えよ。

(1) He's a very (　　　) person, full of energy.

(2) He is the greatest (　　　) expert on French art.

(3) The police were determined to catch him, dead or (　　　).

(4) The most (　　　) reason for the accident was that he was driving too fast.

(5) The two brothers are so (　　　) that I never know which is which.

　　ア alike　　　イ unlike　　　ウ lively

　　エ living　　　オ alive　　　カ likely

4 次の各文の誤りを正せ。ただし，下線部は変えないこと。

(1) I think my son is enough old <u>to take a bus alone</u>.

＿＿＿＿＿＿　→　＿＿＿＿＿＿

(2) When the singer appeared, the many <u>audience</u> shouted for joy.

＿＿＿＿＿＿　→　＿＿＿＿＿＿

(3) I couldn't <u>hardly</u> believe that I was elected chairman.

＿＿＿＿＿＿　→　＿＿＿＿＿＿

(4) Students in Japan are generally respective <u>to their *sempai*</u>.

＿＿＿＿＿＿　→　＿＿＿＿＿＿

19 | 句動詞

🖑 要点整理

❶ 前置詞や副詞を含む 2 語の句動詞

> How did John **account for** being late today？（説明する，占める）

> What religion do you **believe in**？（価値を信じる）

> The car **broke down** after it had gone forty miles.（故障する）

> A fire **broke out** in the kitchen.（起こる）

> The work **calls for** endurance and patience.（要求する）

> Would you **care for** a cup of tea？（望む）

> Jack will have the courage to **carry out** the plan.（実行する）

> Where did you **come across** this old album？（見つける）

> I want to **deal with** this letter before lunch.（処理する）

> Can you **do without** the car tomorrow？（なしで済ます）

> Will you **hand in** your essays at the end of the lesson？（提出する）

> Please **hold on**; I'll see if the doctor is in.（（電話を）切らずに待つ）

> Can you **look after** the baby while we are out？（世話をする）

> I couldn't **make out** the word he said.（理解する）

> Don't you think Jane **takes after** her father？（似ている）

> It is hard to **give up** an old habit.（あきらめる，やめる）

❷ 前置詞や副詞を含む 3 語の句動詞

> **Drop in on** us when you next visit London.（立ち寄る）

> He doesn't **get along with** his landlord.（仲良く付き合う）

> What is a good way to **get rid of** cockroaches？（除去する）

> Please **go on with** your game.（続ける）

> I doubt if he'll **go through with** the task.（やり遂げる）

> Don't walk so fast！I can't **keep up with** you.（ついて行く）

> I'm not **looking forward to** the exam at all.（楽しみに待つ）

❸ 動詞＋名詞＋前置詞

> I **caught sight of** her as she turned the corner.（見かける）

> He's always **finding fault with** others.（あらさがしをする）

> They **made fun of** Jack's haircut.（からかう）

> Don't worry. I'll **take care of** your son.（世話をする）

> He **took part in** the Olympic Games ten years ago.（参加する）

1 次の各文の下線部と最も近い意味を表すものを下から選び，記号で答えよ。

☆ (1) John often used to <u>drop in on</u> me. 　　　　　　　　　　　　（　　　）

　　ア despise 　　　　　イ respect

　　ウ visit 　　　　　　エ disregard

☆ (2) The incident <u>took place</u> at midnight. 　　　　　　　　　　（　　　）

　　ア got 　　　　　　　イ happened

　　ウ became 　　　　　エ met

(3) Mary didn't <u>mention</u> the accident she had seen. 　　　　　（　　　）

　　ア care about 　　　イ make clear

　　ウ refer to 　　　　エ run into

☆ (4) My father never <u>despised</u> the poor. 　　　　　　　　　　（　　　）

　　ア cared for 　　　イ looked down on

　　ウ overlooked 　　エ took care of

(5) We <u>went over</u> the house before deciding whether to buy it. 　（　　　）

　　ア moved 　　　　イ invited

　　ウ inspected 　　エ invented

2 次の各組の英文がほぼ同じ内容になるように，＿＿＿に適当な語を入れよ。

☆ (1) { He is always ready to criticize the work of others.
He is always ready to find ＿＿＿＿＿＿ with the work of others.

☆ (2) { I have decided to be an engineer.
I have made ＿＿＿＿＿ ＿＿＿＿＿ ＿＿＿＿＿ to be an engineer.

☆ (3) { Who will look after the child ?
Who will take ＿＿＿＿＿ of the child ?

(4) { A good idea presented itself in my mind.
A good idea ＿＿＿＿＿ across my mind.

(5) { She was reared in London, and that is why she speaks English fluently.
She was ＿＿＿＿＿ up in London, and that is why she speaks English fluently.

3 次の各文の下線部と最も近い意味を表すものを下から選び，記号で答えよ。 [福井工業大]

(1) We can no longer put up with the present situation. （　　）

(2) You should know it will put out even the last gleam of her hope. （　　）

(3) Just take part in the contest, for this is an excellent chance of displaying your talent.

（　　）

(4) What does SDI stand for ? （　　）

(5) Let's make use of our time wisely, so that we'll be able to finish our work soon.

（　　）

ア improve	イ represent	ウ repair
エ utilize	オ distinguish	カ repeat
キ endure	ク criticize	ケ participate
コ extinguish		

4 次の各文の（　）内に下から適当なものを選び，記号で答えよ。

(1) If you don't have any plans for later tonight, you should (　　　) my house. [金沢工業大]

ア come on　　　イ go on　　　ウ stay up　　　エ stop by

(2) Parents need to stand (　　) for children. [大阪経済大]

ア up　　　イ from　　　ウ of　　　エ at

(3) Surprisingly, military spending used to (　　　) for more than 20% of the GDP in that country.

ア account　　　イ call　　　ウ pass　　　エ settle

(4) I am so busy that I cannot do (　　) the help of a secretary. [(3)・(4)武蔵大]

ア by　　　イ for　　　ウ over　　　エ without

(5) I would like to (　　) in touch although we are apart. [大阪経済大-改]

ア have　　　イ look　　　ウ keep　　　エ call

(6) (　　　) attention to what he says. He is very reliable. [名城大]

ア Make　　　イ Do　　　ウ Pay　　　エ Feel

(7) George finally got (　　　) his serious injury. [畿央大]

ア up　　　イ in　　　ウ out　　　エ over

(8) There's an old bike I'm trying to (　　　). Do you want it ?

ア take after　　　イ get rid of　　　ウ hold on　　　エ go on with

(9) Since Bob was still hungry, he called (　　　) more meat.

　ア for　　　　　　イ at　　　　　　ウ up　　　　　　エ off

(10) My sister has twin sons. They are so alike that I can't (　　　) them apart.

　ア get　　　　　　イ keep　　　　　　ウ live　　　　　　エ tell

5 次の各文の下線部の誤りを正せ。

(1) I've been looking forward to visit Germany during summer vacation.

＿＿＿＿＿＿＿＿＿＿＿＿＿＿＿＿＿＿＿＿＿

(2) Whenever I come upon a word I do not know, I always look it off in the dictionary.

[神奈川大-改]

＿＿＿＿＿＿＿＿＿＿＿＿＿＿＿＿＿＿＿＿＿

(3) In those days, people really believed that nuclear war would break down.

＿＿＿＿＿＿＿＿＿＿＿＿＿＿＿＿＿＿＿＿＿

6 日本語を参考に，(　　)内の語句を並べかえよ。

(1) 多くの日本の学生は大学を卒業するまで親に頼っている。

Many Japanese students (parents / to / rely / support / their / on) them until they graduate from university.

Many Japanese students ＿＿＿＿＿＿＿＿＿＿＿＿＿＿＿＿＿＿＿＿＿

them until they graduate from university.

(2) 私は彼が人のことを悪く言うのを聞いたことがない。

[(1)・(2)追手門学院大]

I have (ill / him / of / speak / heard / never) others.

I have ＿＿＿＿＿＿＿＿＿＿＿＿＿＿＿＿＿＿ others.

(3) 強風で家の屋根を飛ばされた人々もいた。

[九州産業大]

Some people (their houses / blown / by / had / of / off / the roofs) the strong wind.

Some people ＿＿＿＿＿＿＿＿＿＿＿＿＿＿＿＿ the strong wind.

(4) 今日の好天を利用しない手はない。

[獨協大-改]

Today's beautiful (weather / of / must / be / taken / advantage).

Today's beautiful ＿＿＿＿＿＿＿＿＿＿＿＿＿＿＿＿＿.

🖐 要点整理

❶ **原因・理由を表す前置詞**

{ He suffers **from** a severe headache. (ひどい頭痛で苦しむ)

{ He died **from** overwork. (過労で亡くなった)

{ London is famous **for** its fog. (霧で有名)

{ She cried **for** joy at the news. (うれしくて泣いた)

> The accident happened **through** my carelessness. (不注意で)

❷ **結果を表す前置詞**

> She was moved **to** tears. (彼女は感動して涙を流した。)

> **To** my surprise, they elected me chairman. (驚いたことに)

> The rain turned **into** snow. (雨は雪に変わった。)

❸ **目的を表す前置詞**

> What do you use the tool **for**? (何のためにその道具を使うのですか。)

> He travels a great deal **on** business. (仕事で)

❹ **手段・道具を表す前置詞**

> We usually go to school **by** bicycle. (自転車で)

> You must fill out this form **with** a pen. (ペンで)

❺ **分離・はく奪を表す前置詞**

> He is now **off** duty. (彼は今，非番だ。)

> I want to be independent **of** my parents. (私は両親から独立したい。)

❻ **対比・比較を表す前置詞**

> Life is often compared **to** a voyage. (人生はよく航海にたとえられる。)

> My garden is small compared **with**〔**to**〕yours. (あなたの庭に比べて)

❼ **関連・関係を表す前置詞**

> I have nothing to do **with** the matter. (私はその事柄に関係ない。)

> Talk **of** the devil, and he is sure to appear. (うわさをすれば影。)

❽ **付帯状況を表す前置詞**

> Jane was speaking **with** her mouth full of cake.

(ジェーンは口をケーキでいっぱいにしながら話していた。)

❾ **群前置詞**

according to「〜によれば」，as for = as to「〜に関して」，

because of「〜のために」，instead of「〜の代わりに」，

thanks to「〜のおかげで」，with〔for〕al1 = in spite of「〜にもかかわらず」，

by means of「〜を用いて」，in addition to「〜に加えて」，

on account of「〜のために」

1 次の各文の＿＿に適当な前置詞を入れよ。

(1) We talked about our future ＿＿＿＿＿＿ a cup of coffee. 　　　　　　　[高岡法科大-改]

(2) He completed the work ＿＿＿＿＿＿ the cost of his health.

☆ (3) Japan is made up ＿＿＿＿＿＿ four large islands.

☆ (4) Thanks ＿＿＿＿＿＿ your help, I could succeed.

☆ (5) My hat is somewhat different ＿＿＿＿＿＿ yours.

☆ (6) It was very kind ＿＿＿＿＿＿ you to carry the suitcase for me.

(7) He walks seven miles a day ＿＿＿＿＿＿ an average.

☆ (8) We tried to sleep, but the noise kept us ＿＿＿＿＿＿ sleeping.

(9) The car won't go because the engine is ＿＿＿＿＿＿ of order.

☆ (10) She returned safely ＿＿＿＿＿＿ the immense joy of her parents.

☆ **2** 次の各文の適当な位置に，下から適当な語を選んで入れ，全文を書け。ただし，同じ語を2
度使ってもよい。

(1) He had no knife to cut.

＿＿＿＿＿＿＿＿＿＿＿＿＿＿＿＿＿＿＿＿＿＿＿＿＿＿＿＿＿＿＿＿＿＿＿＿＿＿

(2) Nothing peace could save the world.

＿＿＿＿＿＿＿＿＿＿＿＿＿＿＿＿＿＿＿＿＿＿＿＿＿＿＿＿＿＿＿＿＿＿＿＿＿＿

(3) I half believe life after death.

＿＿＿＿＿＿＿＿＿＿＿＿＿＿＿＿＿＿＿＿＿＿＿＿＿＿＿＿＿＿＿＿＿＿＿＿＿＿

(4) I want to find a book American history.

＿＿＿＿＿＿＿＿＿＿＿＿＿＿＿＿＿＿＿＿＿＿＿＿＿＿＿＿＿＿＿＿＿＿＿＿＿＿

(5) The house the roof which you see over there is mine.

＿＿＿＿＿＿＿＿＿＿＿＿＿＿＿＿＿＿＿＿＿＿＿＿＿＿＿＿＿＿＿＿＿＿＿＿＿＿

(6) There is something wrong this computer.

＿＿＿＿＿＿＿＿＿＿＿＿＿＿＿＿＿＿＿＿＿＿＿＿＿＿＿＿＿＿＿＿＿＿＿＿＿＿

(7) I took it granted that he would agree with us.

＿＿＿＿＿＿＿＿＿＿＿＿＿＿＿＿＿＿＿＿＿＿＿＿＿＿＿＿＿＿＿＿＿＿＿＿＿＿

〔of, with, for, on, but, in〕

advice

1 (6)この場合，for は誤り。
(10)「両親がとても喜んだことに」の意味。

3 次の各文の（　）内に下から適当なものを選び，記号で答えよ。

(1) Did you have a chance to meet your grandfather （　　　） the winter vacation ?

［センター試験］

 ア during   イ inside   ウ on   エ while

(2) （　　　） my surprise, I had a lot in common with my new friend.   ［青山学院大］

 ア For   イ In   ウ To   エ With

(3) （　　　） arriving at the scene of the crime, the police discovered the suspect had already gone.   ［学習院大］

 ア As   イ At   ウ On   エ With

(4) I've got to pay the money back （　　） the end of the month.   ［関西学院大］

 ア by   イ on   ウ over   エ till

(5) The professor's explanation was （　　） my understanding.   ［玉川大］

 ア at   イ out   ウ beside   エ beyond

(6) Our company had good sales this year, so the employees' bonuses were increased （　　　） twenty percent.   ［金沢工大］

 ア at   イ by   ウ for   エ on

(7) We will not share any of your personal details with anyone （　　　） for the police.

［関西学院大］

 ア apart   イ despite   ウ except   エ partly

(8) In Japan, meat is usually sold （　　　）.   ［日本女子大］

 ア at the gram イ by the gram ウ for a gram エ in a gram

(9) （　　　） its faults, I believe this is the best work of that writer.

 ア Despite   イ Instead of   ウ In spite   エ Although

(10) When I got off the train, a man caught me （　　　） the arm.   ［名城大］

 ア at   イ by   ウ off   エ from

4 次の各文の下線部と最も近い意味を表すものを下から選び，記号で答えよ。

(1) All at once all the lights in the house went out.

 ア Finally   イ Potentially   ウ Unfortunately   エ Suddenly

(2) The boy has had the flu and a high fever for three days, but now he is getting better by degrees.

 ア cheerfully   イ gradually   ウ quickly   エ completely

(3) <u>For all</u> its efforts, the Japanese soccer team was defeated.

    ア Because of   **イ** Due to   **ウ** In spite of   **エ** Speaking of

(4) Some aspects of new technology brought us <u>nothing but</u> the destruction of the
environment.   [以上，駒澤大]

    ア only   **イ** more than   **ウ** less than   **エ** all

(5) He was very <u>grateful to</u> you for your kind help.   [名城大]

    ア associated with   **イ** content with   **ウ** thankful to   **エ** indifferent to

5 日本語を参考に，（ ）内の語句を並べかえよ。

(1) 次の夏，電力が不足するだろう。

We (short / electric power / be / of / will) next summer.   [椙山女学園大-改]

We _____ next summer.

(2) 多くの日本人学生は忍耐強いので，コンサートチケットのために列に並んで待ちます。

                                    [武庫川女子大]

(are / enough / in line / many Japanese students / patient / to / wait) for concert
tickets.

_____

_____ for concert tickets.

(3) 世の中は，その向こうに多くのチャンスを見いだすことができる扉で満ちている。[関西学院大]

The world (doors / which / find / can / through / full / we / of / is) many opportunities.

The world _____

_____ many opportunities.

(4) 時間が足りなくなったので演目のいくつかを省くことになった。   [立命館大]

Several items in the (cut / due / of / program / the lack / to / were) time.

Several items in the _____ time.

(5) お願いがあるのですが。

(a / ask / may / favor / of / I / you)?

_____?

(6) 彼には急いですべきことがあった。   [成城大-改]

He (an urgent / attend / had / matter / to / to).

He _____.

装丁デザイン　ブックデザイン研究所
本文デザイン　A.S.T DESIGN
編集協力　　　群企画

大学入試　ステップアップ　英文法【標準】

編著者	大学入試問題研究会	発行所	受験研究社
発行者	岡 本 泰 治		
印刷所	ユ ニ ッ ク ス		© 株式会社 増進堂・受験研究社

〒550-0013 大阪市西区新町2丁目19番15号
注文・不良品などについて：(06)6532-1581（代表）／本の内容について：(06)6532-1586（編集）

大学入試 ステップ アップ
STEP UP ↗

Standard
標準

英文法

解答・解説

01 文と文型 (pp. 4〜5)

1 (1) from (2) × (3) of (4) of (5) ×
(6) × (7) to

解説

(1)〈keep〔prevent, stop〕+ 人 + from +〜ing〉「人に
〜させない」

(2) reach = arrive at = get to「〜に着く」

(3)〈remind + 人 + of 〜〉「（物・事）が人に〜を思い
出させる」

(4)〈It is + 性質を表す形容詞 + of + 人 + to 不定詞〉

(5) resemble は他動詞。resemble = take after「〜に
似ている」

(6) discuss = talk about「〜を話し合う」

(7)〈apologize to + 人 + for 〜〉「〜を人に謝罪する」

2 ウ，カ

解説

ア get は第 4 文型(S + V + O + O)をとれる。

イ find は第 5 文型(S + V + O + C)をとれる。it
は形式目的語で，真目的語は to 以下。

ウ say は〈動詞 + 人 + to 不定詞〉の構文をとらない。

エ〈persuade + 人 + to 不定詞〉「人を〜するよう説得
する」

オ become を第 3 文型(S + V + O)で使うと「〜に
似合う」の意味になる。

カ mind は不定詞を目的語にとることはできない。
動名詞 bringing ならば正しい。

3 (1) It is necessary for you
(2) the castle (which〔that〕) I
(3) It is no use reading〔to read〕
such a book.
(4) explain the meaning to you
(5) is it convenient for〔to〕you

解説

(1) necessary, difficult, impossible, easy などは人
を主語にできない。

(2)「訪問する」という意味の visit は他動詞のため，at
は不要。

(3) no use を使った構文は〜ing の目的語を主語とす
ることはできない。

(4) explain は第 4 文型(S + V + O + O)をとれない。

(5) convenient は人を主語にはできない。

4 (1)ア (2)ア，ウ (3)イ (4)ア (5)イ
(6)ア，イ (7)ア

解説

(1) smell「〜なにおいがする」を第 2 文型(S + V + C)
で用いる場合，C は形容詞。

(2)〈promise（+ 人 +）to 〜〉「（人に）〜することを約
束する」，〈promise that + S + V〉の構文が可能。

(3)〈enjoy +（動）名詞〉が可能。

(4) interest を他動詞として用いると，「〜に興味を
持たせる」の意味になる。

(5) introduce は第 4 文型をとることができないため，
「人に〜を紹介する」は〈introduce 〜 to + 人〉で表す。

(6) try to 〜「〜しようと努める」, try 〜ing「〜をやっ
てみる」意味の差はあるが両方の構文が可能。

(7)〈order + 人 + to 不定詞〉「人に〜するよう命令する」

02 時 制 (pp. 6〜7)

1 (1)ア (2)イ (3)エ (4)エ (5)イ
(6)ア (7)ウ (8)エ

解説

(1) does = smokes does は代動詞。

(2)〈must have + 過去分詞〉「〜したに違いない」，過
去の事柄に関する推量を表す。

(5)時や条件を表す副詞節の中では，未来（完了）形の
代用として，現在（完了）形を用いる。

(6)過去のある「時」より前のことを表すには，過去完
了形を用いる。

(7)(5)を参照。

(8)未来のある時点までに完了する事柄とその結果を
表現するには，未来完了形を用いる。

2 (1)ア (2)ア (3)ウ (4)イ (5)ア

解説

(1)条件を表す副詞節内なので，未来形は不可。

(2) since は「過去のある時点から現在まで」を表すた
め，基本的に現在完了（進行）形で用いられる。

(3) resemble「〜に似ている」は進行形不可。

(4) when は時の 1 点を明示する語なので，現在完了
形を用いることはできない。

(5)「私がここに来た」時点までの継続を表すため，過去完了（進行）形にする必要がある。

3 (1) will be snowing when we get to Kanazawa
(2) failed to get the position I had
(3) was sure she would be able to speak French

解説

(1)「～しているでしょう」を未来進行形で表す。
(2)「待ち望んでいた」のは「得られなかった」時点より前なので，had wanted とする。〈fail + to 不定詞〉「～できない」
(3)時制の一致を受けるため，will ではなく would を用いる。will が不要。

03 助動詞 (pp. 8〜9)

1 (1)イ (2)ウ (3)イ (4)ア (5)ア
(6)ア (7)ア (8)ア (9)イ (10)ア

解説

(1)「ダイエット中なので，食べるべきではない」
(2) as ～ as + S + can = as ～ as possible「できるだけ～」
(3)〈used + to 不定詞〉は過去の習慣を表す。be used to ～ing「～するのに慣れている」と混同しないこと。
(4) had better の否定形は had better not ～。
(5)(6) ought to have + 過去分詞 ≒ should have + 過去分詞「～すべきだったのに（しなかった）」
(7) can't have + 過去分詞「～したはずがない」
(8) Let's ～の付加疑問は shall we を用いる。
(9)主語の強い意志を表す。擬人的に無生物にも用いる。「ドアはどうしても開こうとしなかった。」
(10) can't は否定の推量で「～のはずがない」の意。

2 (1) must (2) must, have
(3) can't(cannot) (4) may
(5) I, should (6) will

解説

(1) must「～に違いない」，強い推量を表す。
(2) must have + 過去分詞「～したに違いない」，mistake ... for ～「…を～と間違える」
(3) cannot have + 過去分詞「～したはずがない」
(4) have good reason to ～「～するには十分理由がある」，may well + 原形動詞「～するのは当然だ」
(5)命令・提案・決定の内容を表す that 節の中では should を用いる。

(6) will は習性・習慣を表す場合にも用いられる。「子どもはいたずらなものである。」の意味。
e.g. Accidents *will* happen.（事故は起こるものだ。）

04 不定詞 (pp. 10〜13)

1 (1)ア (2)ア (3)イ (4)イ (5)イ
(6)ウ (7)ア (8)ウ (9)ウ (10)イ

解説

(1) invite 以外は〈V + 人 + to 不定詞〉の構文をとれない。
(2)〈have + 人 + 原形不定詞〉「（人に）～させる」，have は使役動詞。
(3)〈疑問詞 + to ～〉の形。*e.g.* when to leave「いつ出発すべきか」，what to do「何をすべきか」，which to choose「どれを選ぶべきか」
(4) too ... to ～「…すぎて～できない」，to be seen と受け身形にすることに注意。
(5)〈expect + 人 + to ～〉「（人が）～するように期待する」，hope, suggest はこの構文をとることはできない。
(6)〈make + 人 + 原形不定詞〉「無理に（人に）～させる」make は使役動詞。
(7)〈hear（知覚動詞）+ 人 + 原形不定詞〉「（人が）～するのを聞く」
(8)〈want + 人 + to ～〉「（人に）～してほしい」，〈let + 人 + 原形不定詞〉「（人に）～させる」，let は使役動詞。
(9) try not to ～「～しないように努力する」，don't try to ～「～しようと努力しない」の意味の差に注意。
(10)〈形容詞・副詞 + enough not to ～〉の語順に注意。否定語は to ～の直前に置く。

2 (1)ア (2)イ (3)エ

解説

(1)結果を表す不定詞，only to ～「～するだけだった」が適切。
(2) to have been は述語動詞 seems の1つ前の時制，つまり過去（＝若かったとき，～だった）を表す。
(3) can't afford to ～「～する余裕がない」

3 (1) to, return (2) managed
(3) have, only (4) likely, to, have
(5) better, than, to (6) fails, to
(7) enough (8) to (9) To (10) make

解説

(1)結果を表す不定詞。never to ～「決して～しない」
(2) manage to ～「なんとか～する」
(3) have only to ～「～しさえすればよい」
(4) be likely to ～「～であるらしい，～しそうである」

推量・可能性を表す。

(5) know better than to ～「分別があるから～しない」

(6) never fail to ～「必ず～する」

(7)〈so ＋形容詞・副詞 ＋ as to ～〉「とても～なので…」，目的を表す so as to ～「～するために」と混同しないこと。

(8) be to ～の形で〔予定〕，〔義務〕，〔命令〕，〔可能〕，〔運命〕，〔意図〕などの様々な意味を表す。ここでは〔可能〕を表す。

(9) To hear him talk の部分が仮定を表す。「彼が話すのを聞けば」

(10)慣用的独立不定詞。to make matters worse「さらに悪いことに」 *e.g.* to tell the truth「実を言うと」，to begin with「まず第一に」

---

4 (1)ウ (2)イ (3)ウ (4)ア (5)イ (6)エ

解説

(1) to smoke が正しい。be allowed to ～「～するのを許される，～してよい」

(2) effectively が正しい。動詞の原形 reduce にかかるため，形容詞ではなく副詞。

(3) to have been published が正しい。「出版された」のは述語動詞 is より1つ前の時制なので，完了不定詞〈to have ＋過去分詞〉を用いる。

(4) to dance が正しい。〈知覚動詞 ＋ O ＋原形不定詞〉の文が受動態になると，原形不定詞が to 不定詞になる。*e.g.* We saw Mary *dance.* → Mary was seen *to dance.*

(5) get が正しい。あとに to voice とあるが，原形不定詞ではなく to 不定詞をとる使役動詞は get のみ。

(6) a chance to act が正しい。名詞 chance を形容詞的用法の不定詞が修飾している。

---

5 (1) in order to save enough money for
(2) pretend to have had nothing to do with
(3) nice of you to come all the way

解説

(1) in order to ～「～するために」と目的を表す。

(2) pretend to ～「～するふりをする」と，完了不定詞（to have ＋過去分詞）の合成。

(3)〈It is ＋性質を表す形容詞 ＋ of ＋人 ＋ to ～.〉の形。

---

05 動名詞 (pp. 14〜17)

1 (1)ウ (2)ウ (3)エ (4)ウ (5)ア
(6)エ (7)ウ (8)イ (9)ア (10)エ

解説

(1) There is no ～ing「～することは不可能だ」＝ It is impossible to ～で表すことができる。*e.g. There is no knowing* what will happen next. ＝ *It is impossible to know* what will happen next.

(2) be worth ～ing「～する価値がある」

(3) enjoy ～ing「～して楽しむ」

(4) mind ～ing「～することをいやがる」この場合の my dropping の my は動名詞の意味上の主語を表す。drop in on ～「～に立ち寄る」

(5) It is no use ～ing「～することはむだだ」

(6) look forward to ～ing「～することを期待する」

(7)動名詞の意味上の主語は，目的格か所有格で表すが，この場合は文全体の主語なので his が適当である。

(8) need〔want〕～ing「～する必要がある」*e.g.* This car *needs fixing.* ＝ This car *needs to be fixed.*

(9) object to ～ing「～することに反対する」

(10) be busy (in) ～ing「～することに忙しい」

---

2 (1) keeping (2) like (3) no, finding
(4) of, succeeding(success)
(5) without, saying

解説

(3) have difficulty (in) ～ing「～するのが難しい」

(4) be sure of ～ing「(文の主語が)～することを確信している」，be sure to ～「(話し手が)～することを確信している」の意味の差に注意。

(5) It goes without saying that ～「～は言うまでもない」

---

3 (1) have any difficulty getting
(2) no telling which team will win
(3) are not used to doing chores

解説

(1) have difficulty ～ing「～するのに苦労する」

(2) There is no ～ing「～するのは不可能だ」

(3) be used to ～ing「～するのに慣れている」，do chores「雑用をする」

---

4 (1)ア (2)イ (3)ウ (4)イ (5)ウ (6)イ

解説

(1) failing が正しい。前置詞 after の後に置ける準動詞は動名詞。

(2) to reserve が正しい。forget ～ing は「～したの を忘れる」，forget to ～ は「～するのを忘れる」。 sleeping car は「寝台車」の意味で，sleeping は用 途を表す動名詞。

(3) having が正しい。be proud of ～ing の構文で， 動名詞の前に意味上の主語 her son が置かれた形。

(4) eating が正しい。try to ～ は「～しようとする」の 意味で，実際には食べていないことになる。try ～ing「～してみる」が適切。

(5) from が正しい。

(6) causing が正しい。in addition to ＋名詞〔動名詞〕 「～（すること）に加えて」

---

5 (1) to learn → learning
(2) to like → liking
(3) to repair → repairing (to be repaired)
(4) mailing → to mail
(5) to cook → cooking

解説

(1) remember ～ing「～したことを覚えている」
(2) cannot help ～ing ＝〈cannot but ＋動詞の原形〉 「～せざるを得ない」
(3) need〔want，require〕～ing「～する必要がある」
(4) forget ～ing「～したのを忘れる」と forget to ～ 「～するのを忘れる」を区別すること。
(5) be busy ～ing「～することに忙しい」

---

6 (1) me for coming home so late
(2) you mind showing me your passport
(3) was sold on her moving
(4) world-famous for being safe and running on
(5) cannot help feeling sorry for

解説

(1)〈scold ＋人＋ for ～ing〉「（人を）～したことで叱る」
(2) my が不要。「拝見していいですか」→「見せてい ただけますか」と考え，Would you mind ～？「～ していただけますか。」とする。Would you mind my ～ing？「～してもいいですか。」と区別するこ と。
(3) soon が不要。on ～ing「～するとすぐに」
(4) be famous for ～「～で有名である」
(5) cannot help ～ing「～せざるを得ない」

---

06 分詞 (pp. 18～21)

1 (1)エ (2)イ (3)エ (4)ウ (5)ア
(6)イ (7)ウ (8)ウ (9)ウ (10)ウ (11)ウ

解説

(1)〈have ＋ O ＋過去分詞〉「O を～してもらう」ここ では「hair が cut される」の関係が成り立つ。
(2) seem の補語に過去分詞を用いた形。please は他 動詞で「喜ばせる」，過去分詞 pleased で「喜ぶ」の 意味。
(3) keep ＋ O ＋～ing「O を～させたままにする」
(4)否定の分詞構文。
(5)空所以下が後ろから名詞 company を修飾してい る。「ドイツから車を輸入している会社」
(6)「落ちてしまった葉〔落ち葉〕」完了を表す過去分詞。
(7)〈make oneself ＋過去分詞〉「～してもらう」
(8)主語 weather を補った慣用的独立分詞構文。「天 気が許すなら」
(9) dress は他動詞で「着せる」，過去分詞 dressed で 「着ている」の意味。
(10)〈with ＋ O ＋分詞など〉「O を～の状態で」ここで は「legs が cross される」の関係が成り立つ。
(11)「熱帯の気候に慣れている」とあるので，それより 前に，グアムに住んだことがある，または今まで ずっと住んでいる，と考えて分詞の完了形を選ぶ。

---

2 (1) drowned → drowning
(2) shocking → shocked
(3) Having not → Not having
(4) was → being (5) says → said

解説

(1) a drowning man「おぼれている人」
(2) As I was deeply shocked, を分詞構文にする。
(3)分詞構文の否定語は分詞の前に置く。
(4)接続詞を補うか，分詞構文にする。As it was Sunday, the library was closed. も正しい。
(5) it は that 以下を表す形式目的語。said は it を説 明する目的格補語である。We often hear people say that ～. も正しい。

---

3 (1) All, considered
(2) Talking (Speaking), of

解説

どちらも慣用的分詞構文。

4 (1) Not, knowing　(2) Frankly, in
　　(3) him, lying　(4) Admitting
　　(5) There, being, nothing

解説
(1)分詞構文では not は分詞の直前に置く。
(2) frankly speaking「率直に言って」は慣用的独立分
　詞構文。take part in 〜「〜に参加する」
(3)〈find + 目的語 + 現在分詞〉「…が〜しているのを
　見つける」
(4) admitting 〜「〜は認めるけれども」
(5)分詞の意味上の主語と文の主語が違うので，there
　を省略できない。

5 (1) delivered　(2) injured
　　(3) boring　(4) Judging　(5) seated
　　(6) being

解説
(1)〈have + O + 過去分詞〉「O を〜してもらう」
(2) injure は他動詞で「けがをさせる」，過去分詞
　injured で「けがをした」の意味。
(3) bore「人を退屈させる」の意味の他動詞なので
　bored「(人が)退屈している」，boring「(人を)退屈
　させる」となる。
(4) judging from 〜「〜から判断すると」慣用句。
(5) seat は他動詞で「腰かけさせる」の意。seat oneself
　= be seated = sit「腰かける」の意味。the man (who
　was) seated 〜と考える。
(6)分詞の意味上の主語と文の主語が異なるときは，
　分詞の主語は省略しない。

6 (1) bought a lot of used books
　　(2) to discover that the door
　　　remained unclosed
　　(3) early this year, compared with
　　(4) make myself understood in English
　　(5) had a bad tooth pulled out

解説
(1)分詞単独で名詞を修飾するときは，〈分詞 + 名詞〉
　の語順。used book「古本」
(2) remain「〜のままでいる」の補語として過去分詞
　を用いた文。
(3) than が不要。earlier this year than なら正しい。
(4)〈make oneself + 過去分詞〉「〜してもらう」
(5)〈have + 目的語 + 過去分詞〉「…を〜してもらう」
　e.g. I *had* my eyes *examined*.（目を検査してもらっ
　た。）

07 受け身　(pp. 22〜23)

1 (1)イ　(2)ウ　(3)ウ　(4)ウ　(5)イ
　　(6)ウ　(7)ア　(8)エ　(9)ウ　(10)ウ

解説
(1) be located「位置する」
(2)進行形の受動態〈be 動詞 + being + 過去分詞〉の形。
(3) speak to 〜「〜に話しかける」のような句動詞は，
　ひとまとまりで受動態にする。「彼は話しかけら
　れないかぎり，めったに話さない。」
(4) be known as 〜「〜として知られる」，be known
　for 〜「〜で知られる」，be known to 〜「〜に知ら
　れる」を区別すること。
(5) shock は他動詞で「ショックを与える」の意味な
　ので，受動態で「ショックを受ける」となる。
(6) injure は他動詞で「けがをさせる」の意味，受動
　態で「けがをする」。hurtful は「感情を傷つける」。
　wound は「傷つける」なので，be wounded で「傷
　つく」となるが，戦争などで負傷する場合に使わ
　れ，事故のときには使わない。damage は「(物に)
　損害を与える」。
(7) prefer 〜ing「〜するのを好む」と，〈be 動詞 + 過
　去分詞〉を組み合わせた形。
(8) laugh at 〜「〜を笑う」の受動態。「友だち全員に」
　となるため，by も必要。
(9) S is said to 〜「S は〜と言われている」の文。to 以
　下は「言われていた」よりも前の時を表すので，完
　了不定詞。
(10)〈must have + 過去分詞〉「〜したに違いない」と，
　〈be 動詞 + 過去分詞〉を組み合わせた形。

2 (1) held, other　(2) relied(depended)

解説
(1)hold a meeting「会議を開く」, every other week「1
　週おきに」 *cf.* every three weeks「3 週ごとに」

3 (1)ア　(2)ウ　(3)イ　(4)ア

解説
(1) submit は「提出する」なので，be submitted なら
　ば正しい。
(2) deliver は「配達する」なので, delivered ならば正しい。
(3) pleased ならば正しい。pleasant は「(物が)人を
　楽しませる」。
(4) I was surprised to know ならば正しい。

08 比　較 (pp. 24〜25)

1 (1)ウ　(2)ア　(3)ウ　(4)エ　(5)ア
　(6)ウ　(7)イ　(8)ウ　(9)ア　(10)ア

解説

(1) money は不可算名詞なので few は不可。little の
　比較級，less が適切。

(2)比較級を強める語句には much，far，even，a lot
　などがある。**ウ**は more と heavier と，比較級が
　重複する。

(3)〈the ＋序数＋最上級〉「…番目に〜な」

(4)〈the ＋比較級＋ of the two〉「2 人〔2 つ〕の中で〜
　なほう」

(5) prefer 〜 to ...「…よりも〜が好きだ」この to は前
　置詞なので，あとに準動詞を置く場合は動名詞。

(6)「エミリーは美しいというよりかわいい。」1 人〔1
　つ〕の性質を比較する場合，-er とするべき語にも
　more を使う。

(7)差(＝ three years)は比較級の直前に置く。文末
　に by 〜の形で置いてもよい。

(8)倍数表現は as 〜 as ...の直前に twice〔X times〕を置く。

(9)「あの選手は天才というよりはむしろ努力家だ。」
　not so much 〜 as ...「〜というよりはむしろ…」

(10)「7 脚しかいすがなかった」no more than 〜 ＝ only
　〜で，少なさを強調する表現であることに注意。

2 (1)No　(2)better, than
　(3)less　(4)twice, as, as　(5)to
　(6)anything, else

解説

(1)最上級を，原級・比較級を用いて書き換える問
　題は頻出。→ This (river) is *longer than any other*
　river in the world.

(2)know better than to 〜「〜しないだけの分別がある」

(3) no less 〜 than ... は肯定的な意味をもつことに注
　意。「…と比べて決して〜の点で劣ることはない」
　つまり as 〜 as ... と同じ意味になる。

(4)表現の差に注意。*e.g.* The country is *ten times the*
　size of Japan. ＝ The country is *ten times as large as*
　Japan.

(5) than を用いない比較級。

(6)最上級から比較級に。Nothing is more precious than
　time. または Nothing is as precious as time. も可能。

09 関係詞 (pp. 26〜29)

1 (1) when　(2) but　(3) what
　(4) where　(5) why　(6) What(ever)
　(7) what　(8) which　(9) whom　(10) that

解説

(1)先行詞は主語の The time。時を表す関係副詞，
　when が適切。

(2)「時々誤りを犯さない人は，この世には一人もい
　ない。」の意味。否定を含む関係詞 but を用いる。

(3) A is to B what C is to D.「A と B の関係は C と D の
　関係と同じである。」p.26 ②「what の慣用表現」を参照。

(4)場所を表す関係副詞，where が適切。

(5) That is why 〜.「そういうわけで〜。」

(6)ことわざ「やってしまったことは，取り返しがつ
　かない。」

(7) what is more「さらにその上」*cf.* what is better
　〔worse〕「さらに良いことに〔悪いことに〕」p.26 ②
　を参照。

(8)前文の内容，またはその一部を受ける which の用法。

(9)先行詞は人で目的格。

(10)先行詞が everything などのときは，通例 that を
　用いる。

2 (1) whichever　(2) whenever
　(3) Whoever　(4) whomever
　(5) wherever　(6) whatever

解説

(1) whichever「〜のどれでも」

(2) whenever「〜の時はいつでも」

(3) whoever「〜のだれもが」

(4) whomever「〜のだれにでも」

(5) wherever「〜のどこにでも」

(6) whatever「〜の何でも」

3 (1) that → which　(2) what → that(as)
　(3) whomever → whoever
　(4) which → in which(where)
　(5) that → which　(6) that → whom

解説

(1) that は継続用法には用いられない。

(2) the same があるので，通例 that を用いる。

(3)主格なので whoever が適切。

(4) Washington was born in the house. → in which(＝
　where) Washington was born の関係である。

(5)前文の内容を受けているため，which が正しい。

(6)〈前置詞＋関係代名詞〉では，that は用いられない。

4 (1)ア　(2)ウ　(3)ウ　(4)イ　(5)イ

解説

(2)主格の複合関係代名詞。

(3)前文の内容を受ける関係形容詞 in which case は「そしてその場合」の意味になる。

(4) what with ... and ～「…やら～やらで」慣用句。

(5) ... at Central High School, and it (= the school) is close to the Palace の下線部の代名詞 it を関係詞で置き換えるのだから，which が適切。where は不可。

5 (1)エ　(2)ウ　(3)ウ　(4)ア　(5)イ
　　(6)ア　(7)イ　(8)ウ　(9)ウ　(10)ウ　(11)イ

解説

(1) where〔to which〕you would like to go または〔(which〔that〕) you would like to go to ならば正しい。

(2)意味の上では I like *it* best なので，目的格の関係代名詞 which〔that〕ならば正しい。

(3) was stolen までが主部，reported が文の動詞なので，who がなければ正しい。

(4)意味の上では I thought *he* was a friend なので，主格の who〔that〕ならば正しい。

(5)先行詞がないので，what ならば正しい。

(6) Whenever ならば正しい。「質問のあるときはいつでも」

(7)意味の上では neither of *them* なので，目的格 whom ならば正しい。

(8) what ならば正しい。〈what + S + used to be〉「以前の～」

(9)文の補語になる節を作る接続詞なので，that ならば正しい。

(10) what ならば正しい。which〔that〕を使う場合は，the cost of a barrel of oil が先行詞として必要。

(11) which ならば正しい。関係詞の継続用法に that を用いることはできない。

10 仮定法　(pp. 30～31)

1 (1)エ　(2)ウ　(3)イ　(4)エ
　　(5)ア　(6)イ　(7)ア　(8)ア

解説

(1)現在の事実に反する仮定は，主節は過去の助動詞を用いる。

(2) If a severe earthquake should happen, ... ? の If を省略しての倒置。

(3)従属節は過去完了形であるが，主節は現在の事実

に反する仮定であるから，過去の助動詞を用いる。

(4)過去の事実に反する仮定。

(5) If it had not been for ～「(過去のある時点に)～がなかったならば」，If it were not for ～は現在の事実に反する仮定に用いる。

(6) without ～ = but for ～「～なしには」の意味。

(7)慣用句 as if ～ = as though ～「まるで～かのように」

(8) insist は「主張する」。命令・提案を表す that 節内では，動詞は〈(should +)原形〉となる。

2 (1)But, for　(2)With　(3)had, taken
　　(4)If　(5)it　(6)wish, could

解説

(1) but for ～ = without ～この場合，If it had not been for ～にも言い換えられる。

(2)条件を表す with「～があれば」

(3)過去の事実に反する仮定なので，過去完了形を用いる。

(4) If only ～「～でありさえすれば」I wish を用いても同じ内容を表せる。

(5) If it were not for ～の If を省略し，Were it not for ～と倒置した用法。

(6) I wish ～「～であればなあ」*e.g. I wish* I had worked harder when I was at college.(大学のときに，もっと一生懸命に勉強しておけばよかったなあ。)

11 話法・時制の一致　(pp. 32～33)

1 (1)told, was, me, him
　　(2)asked, he, was
　　(3)he, had, bought, that, before
　　(4)asked, not, to, forget
　　(5)suggested(proposed), we, should

解説

直接話法は，言葉をそのまま相手に伝える言い方。間接話法は，その内容を自分の立場で言い直して伝える言い方。

(1)被伝達文が平叙文なので said to → told

(2)被伝達文が疑問文なので，〈asked + 人 + 疑問詞 + S + V〉とする。

(3)時制の一致を受けて，bought → had bought とする。

(4)被伝達文が please を伴った命令文なので，asked + 人 + (not) to ～とする。please のない命令文であれば told + 人 + (not) to ～とする。

(5)被伝達文が，人を勧誘する文なので said (to ～) → suggested〔proposed〕(that ～) とする。

2 (1) said, Wait, I, return
(2) said, Have, you
(3) You, had, here, tomorrow
(4) said, Let's, tomorrow
(5) Who, do, you, think, is

解説
(2) if 節は単純疑問文（疑問詞のない疑問文）に直す。
(3) had better は仮定法に由来する表現なので時制の影響を受けない。
(5) they thought は挿入句である。

3 (1) goes　(2) ended　(3) is
(4) were(was)

解説
(1) that 節の内容が不変の真理なので，時制の影響を受けず，常に現在形。
(2) 歴史的事実なので，時制の一致は受けず，常に過去形。ended を had ended としないこと。
(3) than 以下は現在の事実なので，現在形でよい。
(4) 仮定法は時制の影響を受けない。

4 (1) tells me that if I don't sleep well, I can't focus on my studies
(2) feel like walking to a restaurant, ask if they have "demae" which means home

解説
(1) 間接話法の文。that 節内にさらに if 節と主節がある点に注意。
(2) ask 以下の if 節は「～かどうか」を表す間接疑問。

12 否　定　(pp. 34〜35)

1 (1)ア　(2)イ　(3)ウ　(4)ア　(5)ウ

解説
(1) be far from ～「決して～ではない」*e.g.* His report is *far from* satisfactory.（彼の報告は決して満足のいくものではない。）
(2) hardly ever で「めったに～ない」（= seldom）
(3) Do you mind if ～？の原義は「もし～したらいやですか」なので，否定文で答えると承諾を表す。ここでは「たばこの煙が嫌いです」とあるため，拒否を表すものを選ぶ。〈would rather ＋仮定法過去〉「～のほうがよい」
(4) I'm afraid not. = I'm afraid I cannot lend you a few

dollars. I'm afraid は「残念ですが～」の意味。
(5)「冬に山に登るときは，注意してもしすぎることはない。」*e.g.* We *cannot* be *too* careful in driving a car.

2 (1) last　(2) don't　(3) few
(4) anything　(5) Nobody
(6) without, quarreling(quarrelling)
(7) nothing　(8) none

解説
(1) the last person to ～「決して～しない人」
(2) Why don't you ～ ?「～したらどうですか」
(3) a man of few words「口数の少ない人」
(4) anything but ～「決して～ではない」
(5)「だれがそんな不誠実な政治家を信じることができるだろうか。」修辞疑問文 Who can ～ ? は Nobody can ～. と同じ意味。
(6) never ... without ～ing「～することなしに決して…しない」の二重否定。
(7) have nothing to do with ～「～と全くかかわりがない」，have something to do with ～「～とかかわりがある」
(8) be second to none「だれにも引けをとらない」

3 (1) nothing, but　(2) none
(3) no, means　(4) either

解説
(1)〈do nothing but ＋動詞の原形〉「～するばかりである」
(2) 慣用句。*cf.* Mind your own *business*.（いらぬ世話をするな。）
(3) by no means「決して～ではない」
(4) either は否定語と共に用いて，「…もまた～でない」の意味。*e.g.* If you don't go, I won't either.（君が行かないなら，ぼくも行かない。）

13 無生物主語・名詞構文　(pp. 36〜37)

1 (1) give(bring), you
(2) of, success(succeeding)
(3) pride, her　(4) he, will, recover
(5) minutes', walk
(6) prevented(kept, stopped), from, going
(7) What　(8) Why

解説
(1)「少し散歩すれば，食欲が出るでしょう。」

(2)「私は，彼はきっと成功すると思っている。」

(3)「彼女はプライドの高い人なので，彼に素直に謝ることができなかった。」

(4)「彼には回復の望みはない。」

(5)「5分も歩けば，その湖に着くよ。」

(6)「雨で，山に行けなかった。」

(7)「どのようにして，この結論に達したのですか。」

(8)「なぜあなたは失望しているのですか。」

---

2 (1) Her illness compelled(forced)her to stop studying.

(2) I was astonished at(by) his success.

(3) Rain prevented(kept, stopped) us from going on a picnic last Sunday.

(4) This road will take(bring) you to the station.

解説

(1) compel の代わりに force も可。動名詞を用いると，Her illness prevented〔kept, stopped〕her from studying. となる。

(2)〈be astonished at〔by〕+ 名詞句〉「～を聞いて〔見て〕驚く」

(3) prevent の代わりに，keep, stop なども用いられる。

(4) This road will *lead* you to the station. も可。

---

3 (1) shows what Japan used to be like

(2) medicine will make you feel better

(3) Astonishment deprived me of my power

(4) Gargling every day will keep you from catching colds.

解説

(1) how が不要。what A is like「A がどんな様子か」の意味。*e.g. What is* the weather *like* ?「天気はどうですか。」

(2)〈make ＋ 人 ＋ feel better〉「人の気分を良くする」

(3)〈deprive ＋ 人 ＋ of ～〉「人の～を奪う」

(4)〈keep ＋ 人 ＋ from ～ing〉「人に～させない」, gargle「うがいをする」

---

14 呼応・倒置・強調・省略 (pp.38〜39)

1 (1)エ (2)ア (3)ア (4)ウ (5)イ

解説

(1) You suppose they went □? yesterday. が疑問文になったもの。主節が疑問形になっているので，they went はそのまま。

(2) We decided to return because he was ill. の強調構文。

(3) 否定語を文頭に出すと，その後の語順は疑問文と同じになる。

(4) 質問文に合わせ，have で答える。〈Neither ＋ 助動詞〔be 動詞〕＋ S.〉「S も～ではない。」

(5) 否定文には，肯定の付加疑問をつける。

---

2 (1) wants (2) is (3) takes (4) his (5) is

解説

(1) neither A nor B が主語の場合, 動詞は B に一致する。

(2) 主語は The number なので単数扱い。

(3) part(s) of ～の後の名詞が単数の場合は，通例単数扱い。

(4) each, everyone などは単数扱いで，所有格は his。

(5) Ten dollars は 1 つの単位としてとらえられているので，単数扱い。

---

3 (1)エ (2)エ (3)ウ (4)ウ

解説

(1) 命令・要求・提案・決定などを表す that 節の中で should を用いるが，米語用法では省略可能。

(2) *e.g.* at my uncle's (house), at a baker's (shop)

(3)〈help ＋ 人 ＋ (to)～〉の形式で to を省略するのは米語用法に多く見られる。

(4) 口語では，that をよく省略する。

---

4 (1) not, until, that, arrived

(2) No, had, than

解説

(1) 強調構文はその強調する部分を It is □ that ～. の □ の位置に入れる。*e.g.* He broke the vase on purpose. → It was *the vase* that he broke on purpose.(彼がわざと割ったのはその花びんだ。)

(2) 類似の表現として，Scarcely〔Hardly〕had he gone to bed before〔when〕he fell asleep.(彼はベッドに入るとすぐにぐっすりと寝入った。)がある。

15 接続詞 (pp. 40〜41)

1 (1)ウ (2)イ (3)イ (4)ウ (5)ア
(6)エ (7)ウ

解説

(1) during は前置詞なので，不適当。during his stay in France なら可。
(2) now that 〜「もう〜なのだから」
(3) until〔till〕は否定語と共に，not ... until〔till〕〜「〜するまでは…しない，〜して初めて…する」
(4) as long as 〜「〜の限りは」*e.g.* What do I care *as long as* he keeps out of my way?（彼が邪魔さえしなければ私が何を気にすることがあろうか。）
(5) whenever「〜の時はいつも」
(6) unless = if ... not 〜「〜しなければ」
(7)前文の内容を受けて「そうでなければ」の意味。

2 (1) Though(Although) (2) so
(3) and (4) if (5) until(till)

解説

(1) in spite of 〜「〜にもかかわらず」
(2) so that + S + can〔may〕〜「S が〜するために」目的を表す副詞節。
(3)命令文，and /or 〜「…せよ，そうすれば / さもないと〜」
(4) Do you mind if 〜 ?「もし〜すればいやですか」，つまり，「〜してもいいですか」の意味。
(5)「その赤ちゃんは食事を与えられて初めて，泣きやんだ。」The baby didn't stop crying until he was fed. の強調構文。

3 (1) as (2) moment(minute) (3) order

解説

(1)〈according to + 名詞句〉=〈according as + S + V 〜〉「〜に従って，〜に応じて」
(2) in a moment〔minute〕「すぐに」，the moment〔minute〕〜「〜するとすぐに」
(3) out of order「故障して」，in order that + S + can〔may〕〜「S が〜するために」目的を表す副詞節。

16 名詞・冠詞 (pp. 42〜43)

1 (1)ウ (2)エ (3)ウ (4)ア (5)ウ
(6)ウ (7)エ (8)イ (9)イ (10)イ

解説

(1)〈such a(n) + 形容詞 + 名詞〉=〈so + 形容詞 + a(n) + 名詞〉の冠詞の位置に注意。
(2)〈the + 形容詞〉「〜な人々」
(3) snow は不可算名詞。
(4) in one's twenties/thirties「20/30 歳代で」
(5) hold the line「電話を切らずにおく」
(6) have a good command of 〜「〜（外国語など）を自在に使える」が原義。
(7) get an appointment「約束をする」面会などの「約束」は appointment。
(8) audience, population などは，small, large で修飾する。1 つの単位としてみれば，単数扱い。個々の成員を考えると複数扱い。
(9)店の得意客は customer，家の客は guest。
(10) advice は不可算名詞。lots of〜の lot は名詞なので however では修飾できない。

2 (1)エ (2)イ (3)ア (4)エ (5)エ
(6)エ (7)エ (8)ウ

解説

(1)既出の名詞なので定冠詞 the ならば正しい。
(2) importance（名詞）ならば正しい。
(3) information は不可算名詞。s をとれば正しい。
(4) the hand ならば正しい。〈catch + 人 + by the + 体の部位〉とするのがふつう。
(5) by air「航空便で」ならば正しい。
(6) furniture は不可算名詞。s をとれば正しい。
(7) room は「余地」の意味だと不可算名詞。s をとれば正しい。
(8) difficult を名詞の difficulty にすれば正しい。

17 代名詞 (pp. 44〜45)

1 (1)エ (2)イ (3)ウ (4)イ (5)ウ
(6)ア (7)エ (8)ア (9)ア (10)ア (11)イ

解説

(1)この主語 you は複数なので，再帰代名詞も複数形の yourselves が適切。
(2) money は不可算名詞。
(3)ことわざ。「天は自ら助ける者を助ける。」those who〜「〜する人々」
(4)前出の名詞（= population）を指し，かつ前置詞 of

を伴う場合，代名詞は that〔those〕を用いる。

(5) most の後ろにくる名詞には，the，my，these などの限定詞はつけない。most of の後ろにくる名詞には限定詞が必要。

(6) I am very happy. とほぼ同じ意味。〈抽象名詞＋itself〉= very ＋形容詞

(7) 3 人いる姉妹から 1 人を除いた 2 人を指している。代名詞 other(s) は「残りすべて」を表す場合，the を伴う。

(8) 形式目的語。it は to 以下を指す。

(9) as such「そのように」，such は a gentleman を受けている。

(10) ことわざ。「共同責任は無責任。」

(11) rice は不可算名詞なので，one で受けることはできない。また，生産地を〈of ＋国名〉では表現できない。

2 (1) another　(2) All　(3) nothing
　　(4) nothing　(5) it

解説

(1) one と another は相関的に用いられる。A is one thing; B is another.（A と B は全く別物である）

(2) All you have to do is (to) ～「～しさえすればよい」は，慣用的表現。

(4) nothing but A「A だけ」

(5) it は that 以下を表す形式目的語，said は目的格補語で過去分詞である。

18 形容詞・副詞　(pp. 46〜47)

1 (1) エ　(2) ア　(3) ア　(4) ウ　(5) ウ
　　(6) ア　(7) ア

解説

(1) almost と most を混同しない。almost は副詞なので almost of the boys, almost boys などと言うことはできない。all を修飾する形の**エ**が正しい。

(2) much は比較級，最上級，too を修飾できる。

(3) not～ any = no

(4) pleased「(人が)喜んでいる」，pleasant「(物・事が)楽しい」，pleasing「(人を)楽しくさせる」

(5) busy「(電話回線が)混んでいる」，the line is busy「話し中」

(6) literal「字義通りの」，literary「文学の」，literate「読み書きのできる」

(7) every other day「1 日おきに」*e.g.* every three days「3 日ごとに」= every third day

2 (1) soft　(2) imaginary　(3) Fortunately

解説

(1) 動詞 feel の補語なので，形容詞が適切。

(2) 文脈より，「想像上の」が適切。imaginable「想像できる」，imaginative「想像力に富んだ」と区別する。

(3)「幸運にも」ここでは文全体を修飾する副詞。

3 (1) ウ　(2) エ　(3) オ　(4) カ　(5) ア

解説

(1) lively「活発な」

(2) living「生きている」

(3) alive「生きている」は限定用法では使われない。

(4) likely「ありそうな」

(5) alike「似ている」

4 (1) enough old → old enough
　　(2) many → large　(3) couldn't → could
　　(4) respective → respectful

解説

(1) enough が形容詞・副詞を修飾する場合，その後ろに置く。

(2) audience や population は large/small で多少を表す。

(3) hardly「ほとんど～ない」には，それ自体に否定の意味がある。

(4) respective は「それぞれの」，respectful は「敬意を表する」。

19 句動詞　(pp. 48〜51)

1 (1) ウ　(2) イ　(3) ウ　(4) イ　(5) ウ

解説

(1) drop in(on ＋人 /at ＋場所)「(人 / 場所を)訪ねる」

(2) take place「起こる」

(3) refer to ～「～に言及する」

(4) look down on ～「～を軽べつする」

(5) go over ～「～を調べる」

2 (1) fault　(2) up, my, mind
　　(3) care　(4) came　(5) brought

解説

(1) criticize ～「～を批判する」= find fault with ～

(2) decide「決心する」= make up one's mind

(3) look after ～「～の世話をする」= take care of ～

(4) present itself in one's mind「心に浮かぶ」= come

across one's mind

(5) rear ～「～を育てる」= bring up ～

---

3 (1)キ (2)コ (3)ケ (4)イ (5)エ

解説

(1) put up with ～「～をがまんする」= endure ～
(2) put out ～「～を消す」= extinguish ～
(3) take part (in ～)「(～に)参加する」= participate (in ～)
(4) stand for ～「～を表す」= represent ～
(5) make use of ～「～を利用する」= utilize ～

---

4 (1)エ (2)ア (3)ア (4)エ (5)ウ
(6)ウ (7)エ (8)イ (9)ア (10)エ

解説

(1) stop by ～「～に立ち寄る」
(2) stand up for ～「～を守る」
(3) account for ～「～を占める」, military spending「軍事費」
(4) do without ～「～なしで済ます」
(5) keep in touch (with ～)「(～と)連絡を取り合う」
(6) pay attention to ～「～に注意を払う」
(7) get over ～「～を乗り越える, ～から立ち直る」
(8) get rid of ～「～を処分する, 除去する」
(9) call for ～「～を要求する」
(10) tell ～ apart「～を区別する」

---

5 (1) to visiting (2) up in (3) out

解説

(1) look forward to ～「～を楽しみにする」の to は前置詞。
(2) look ～ up in ...「～(単語など)を…で調べる」
(3) break down「故障する」, break out「起こる」

---

6 (1) rely on their parents to support
(2) never heard him speak ill of
(3) had the roofs of their houses blown off by
(4) weather must be taken advantage of

解説

(1) rely on ～「～に頼る」
(2)〈hear + O + 原形〉「O が～するのを聞く」の文型にする。speak ill of ～「～のことを悪く言う」
(3)〈have + O + 過去分詞 + by ...〉「…に O を～される」の文。blow off「吹き飛ばす」
(4) take advantage of ～「～を利用する」の受動態。

---

20 前置詞 (pp. 52～55)

1 (1) over (2) at (3) of (4) to
(5) from〔to, than〕 (6) of (7) on
(8) from (9) out (10) to

解説

(1) over a cup of coffee「コーヒーを飲みながら」
(2) at the cost of one's health「健康を犠牲にして」
(3) be made up of ～ = consist of ～「～で構成されている」
(4) thanks to ～「～のおかげで」
(5) be different from〔to, than〕～「～と異なる」
(6) kind は人の性質・性格を表す語なので, to 不定詞の意味上の主語は of で表す。
(7) on (an〔the〕) average「平均して」
(8)〈keep + 人 + from ～ing〉「(人を)～させない」
(9) out of order「故障して」↔ in order「調子がよくて」
(10) to her parents' immense joy〈to one's + 感情を表す名詞〉「～なことに」の形式も可能。

---

2 (1) He had no knife to cut with.
(2) Nothing but peace could save the world.
(3) I half believe in life after death.
(4) I want to find a book on American history.
(5) The house the roof of which you see over there is mine.
(6) There is something wrong with this computer.
(7) I took it for granted that he would agree with us.

解説

(1) with a knife「ナイフで」から考える。
(2) nothing but ～ = only ～「～だけ」
(3) believe in ～「～の存在を信じる」
(4) on「(専門的な内容)について」
(5) the roof of the house → the roof of which と考える。
(6) There is something wrong with ～「～に具合の悪いところがある」
(7) take ～ for granted「～を当然のことと思う」it は that 以下を表す形式目的語。

3 (1)ア (2)ウ (3)ウ (4)ア (5)エ
(6)イ (7)ウ (8)イ (9)ア (10)イ

解説
(1)「冬休み中に」。あとに名詞があるため，前置詞 during「〜の間に」が適切。while は接続詞。
(2)「驚いたことに」
(3) on 〜ing「〜するとすぐに」
(4)この by は期限を表す。「月の終わりまでに」
(5)「私の理解をこえて」
(6)差を表す by の用法。*e.g.* older by three years「3 歳年上」
(7) except for 〜「〜のほかは」
(8)「グラム単位で」
(9) despite 〜 = in spite of 〜「〜にもかかわらず」
(10)つかむ，引っ張るなどの動詞では〈動詞＋人＋ by the ＋体の一部〉の形がよく用いられる。

4 (1)エ (2)イ (3)ウ (4)ア (5)ウ

解説
(1)「とつぜん」
(2)「しだいに」
(3)「〜にもかかわらず」
(4)「〜だけ，〜にすぎない」この but は「〜を除いて」を意味する前置詞。
(5)「〜に感謝して」

5 (1) will be short of electric power
(2) Many Japanese students are patient enough to wait in line
(3) is full of doors through which we can find
(4) program were cut due to the lack of
(5) May I ask a favor of you
(6) had an urgent matter to attend to

解説
(1) short of 〜「〜が不足して」
(2) in line「一列に並んで」
(3) we can find many opportunities *through them*(＝*the doors*)から考える。
(4) due to 〜「〜のために」
(5)〈ask ＋人＋ a favor〉＝〈ask a favor of ＋人〉
(6)〈attend 〜〉は「〜に出席する」だが，〈attend to 〜〉は「〜に対応する」の意味になる。